Ready, Steady, Spaghetti

cooking for kids and with kids

Ready, Steady, Spaghetti

cooking for kids and with kids

Lucy Broadhurst

**Andrews McMeel
Publishing, LLC**

Kansas City

contents

read this first...

Cooking is great fun, but before you rush into the kitchen, take a bit of time to get organized. There aren't many rules to cooking but there is a golden one: always read RIGHT TO THE END OF THE RECIPE before you start. Can you imagine how annoying it would be to get to step 4 of your recipe and then have to bribe your little brother to run to the store for a missing ingredient? So, read all the way through and get out all the ingredients and equipment you're going to need.

Chop or shred any ingredients you can before you start. Open cans and wash vegetables or fruit. Grease or line any baking pans you're going to need.

When you've been cooking for a while, you will be able to estimate quantities fairly

accurately; but until then, measure carefully, especially when you're baking. You'll see that there are two scales for measuring: imperial and cup measures. A cup measure is a standard 8 fl oz. Spoon measures are always level, never heaped (unless the recipe specifically says so).

If you're using the oven, arrange the shelves to the correct height before you turn it on. And preheat it before putting things in to cook — the oven will probably have a light to show when it's reached the right temperature. If you put things in the oven and then switch it on to warm up, the food will dry out, and won't be cooked when the recipe says it should be. If you have a fan-forced oven, the temperature will be a bit hotter than a normal oven. The temperature in each recipe is for a normal oven. If you use fan-forced, you don't need to preheat the oven, but you will need to set the temperature to about 18°F lower than the recipe says.

All of the recipes have photographs so you can see what your finished dish is going to look like. Don't worry too much if it doesn't look exactly the same . . . the taste is what matters, not the appearance! Some recipes have step photographs, too, so you can check any tricky techniques as you go.

Nutrition

Before you start cooking, it's a good idea to know how food works in your body. There are five different food groups — protein, carbohydrate, fiber, fat, and vitamins and minerals — all of which play different roles. Proteins, such as meat, fish, dairy (cheese, milk, and eggs), legumes, and nuts, will build your muscles and help you grow. Protein also takes longer to digest, so can keep you feeling full for longer and prevent snacking — that's why it's a good idea to include some protein in your breakfast. Carbohydrates, such as bread, potatoes, rice, and pasta, give you energy. Fiber keeps your insides working properly. Fat, in small amounts, is still an important nutrient, especially for bodies that are growing. Fats from oily fish, nuts, legumes, avocado, and olive oil are the best fats to include regularly. Eating the right amounts of each group will leave you feeling fit and healthy, with plenty of energy, will help your body to stay at its correct weight, and, for children, help your body grow and develop properly. Eating healthily is a matter of following a balanced diet. If you eat three good meals and get vitamins from plenty of fruit and vegetables on most days, then you can afford to indulge in party food on your friends' birthdays.

Hygiene and safety

1 Always ask an adult for permission before you start to cook. And always ask for help if you are not confident with chopping or handling hot pans. An adult must always be present if the recipe involves deep-frying.

2 Before you start, wash your hands well with soap and water, tie back long hair, and wear an apron to protect your clothes.

3 When you're cooking on the stovetop, turn pan handles to the side so there's no danger of knocking them as you walk past. When you're stirring, hold the pan handle firmly. Always use thick, dry oven gloves when you're getting things out of the oven.

4 Chicken should be treated with care, as it can harbor salmonella bacteria. Keep it in the fridge for no more than 2 days, or freeze it for up to 6 months. Once you've thawed chicken, you can't freeze it again unless you cook it first. When you've chopped raw chicken, wash the chopping board and knife before you prepare other ingredients that aren't going to be cooked (such as salad ingredients).

5 Wash up as you go along. This will save hours of cleaning at the end and will keep your work space clear.

little food

berry couscous

SERVES 4 TO 6

1 cup instant couscous

2 cups apple-cranberry juice

1 cinnamon stick

2 cups frozen raspberries, thawed

1²/₃ cups frozen blueberries, thawed

2 teaspoons shredded orange zest

1²/₃ cups strawberries, halved

³/₄ cup plain yogurt, to serve

1 Put the couscous in a bowl. Pour the juice in a saucepan and add the cinnamon stick. Cover and bring to a boil. Pour over the couscous.

2 Cover with plastic wrap and leave for about 5 minutes, or until all the liquid has disappeared. Remove the cinnamon stick from the bowl.

3 Gently pat the thawed berries with paper towels to dry them. Fluff the grains of couscous with a fork, then gently fold in the orange zest and most of the berries.

Spoon into four serving bowls and sprinkle with the remaining berries. Serve with a dollop of yogurt.

french toast

SERVES 2

2 eggs

1 cup whole milk

1/2 teaspoon vanilla extract

3 tablespoons butter

4 thick slices day-old bread

ground cinnamon and sugar, to serve

1 Break the eggs into a wide, shallow dish and add the milk and vanilla extract. Beat with a fork or wire whisk until well mixed.

2 Melt half the butter in a skillet. When the butter begins to bubble, quickly dip a piece of bread into the egg mixture, let the excess run off, then place it in the skillet.

3 Cook for 1 to 2 minutes. When it is golden underneath, turn the bread over and cook the other side.

4 Transfer the French toast to a plate and cover with aluminum foil to keep warm while you cook the rest. Add more butter to the skillet as needed and cook the remaining bread. Serve sprinkled with cinnamon and sugar.

ham and corn muffins

MAKES 24

1 cup self-rising flour

1/4 cup chopped ham

1/3 cup canned corn kernels, drained

1/4 red bell pepper, seeded and finely chopped

2 teapoons chopped Italian parsley

4 tablespoons unsalted butter, melted

1/2 cup whole milk

1 egg

1 tablespoon sesame seeds

1 Preheat the oven to 425°F. Brush 24 mini muffin cups with oil. Sift the flour into a large bowl. Add the ham, corn, pepper, and parsley, and stir to combine.

2 Mix the melted butter, milk, and egg in a bowl. Make a well in the center of the flour mixture and add the milk mixture. Mix the dough lightly until the ingredients are just combined.

3 Spoon the mixture into the muffin cups and sprinkle with the sesame seeds. Bake for 15 to 20 minutes, or until golden.

berry muffins

MAKES 16

1 cup plain yogurt

1 cup rolled oats

3 tablespoons oil

1/3 cup sugar

1 egg

1 cup self-rising flour, sifted

3 teaspoons baking powder

1 1/3 cups frozen mixed berries, thawed

1 Preheat the oven to 350°F. Line 16 standard muffin cups with paper liners. Mix the yogurt, oats, oil, sugar, and egg in a bowl. Gently stir in the sifted flour and baking powder with the berries.

2 Spoon the batter into the paper liners. Bake for 20 to 25 minutes, or until the muffins are golden brown.

blueberry pancakes

2 cups all-purpose flour

2 teaspoons baking powder

1 teaspoon baking soda

1/3 cup sugar

2 eggs

1/3 cup unsalted butter, melted

1 1/4 cups whole milk

2 cups blueberries,
fresh or frozen

honey and plain yogurt, to serve (optional)

1 Sift the flour, baking powder, and baking soda into a large bowl. Add the sugar and make a well in the center. Add the eggs, melted butter, and milk to the dry ingredients, stirring just to combine (add more milk if you prefer a thinner batter).

2 Gently fold the blueberries into the batter (leave some out for serving). Heat a skillet and brush lightly with melted butter or oil. Drop tablespoons of batter into the skillet and cook over low heat until bubbles appear and pop on the surface.

3 Turn the pancakes over and cook the other side (these pancakes can be difficult to handle so take care when turning). Transfer to a plate and cover with a cloth to keep warm while you cook the rest of the batter. Serve warm with some blueberries, a drizzle of honey, and plain yogurt.

scrambled eggs

SERVES 2

4 eggs

3 tablespoons whole milk

1 tablespoon butter

toast or English muffins, to serve

1 In a bowl, beat the eggs and milk lightly with a fork.

2 Melt the butter in a heavy-bottomed skillet over very low heat and pour in the egg mixture. Stir constantly with a wooden spoon, lifting the mixture from the bottom of the skillet so that it cooks evenly. The eggs are ready when they are just set but are still creamy.

3 Remove from the heat and serve immediately on toast or English muffins.

hummus

SERVES 4

1 cup dried chickpeas

4 tablespoons olive oil, plus extra to drizzle

3 to 4 tablespoons lemon juice

2 garlic cloves, crushed

2 tablespoons tahini

1 tablespoon ground cumin

crackers, to serve

1 Soak the chickpeas in water for 8 hours, or overnight. Drain. Put in a saucepan and cover with cold water. Bring to a boil and cook for 50 to 60 minutes. Drain, keeping a cupful of the cooking liquid.

2 Put the chickpeas in a food processor with the oil, lemon juice, garlic, tahini, and cumin. Blend well until the mixture starts to look thick and creamy. With the motor running, gradually add the cooking liquid until the mixture is as thick or thin as you like it. Transfer to a bowl and drizzle with olive oil. Serve with crackers, raw or cooked vegetables, or use as a spread for sandwiches.

tzatziki

SERVES 12

2 small cucumbers

1²/₃ cups low-fat plain yogurt

4 garlic cloves, crushed

3 tablespoons finely chopped mint

1 tablespoon lemon juice

raw vegetables, to serve

1 Cut the cucumbers in half lengthwise and scoop out the pits. Leave the skin on and coarsely grate the cucumbers into a colander. Sprinkle with salt and leave over a large bowl for 15 minutes to drain off any bitter juices.

2 Stir together the yogurt, garlic, mint, and lemon juice in a bowl.

3 Rinse the cucumber under cold water then, taking small handfuls, squeeze out any excess moisture. Mix the grated cucumber with the yogurt. Serve with raw vegetables.

dhal

SERVES 4 TO 6

1¼ cups red lentils

2 tablespoons unsalted butter

1 onion, finely chopped

2 garlic cloves, crushed

1 teaspoon grated fresh ginger

1 teaspoon ground turmeric

1 teaspoon garam masala

pita bread, to serve

1. Put the lentils in a large bowl and cover with water. Remove any floating particles and drain the lentils.

2. Heat the butter in a saucepan. Fry the onion for about 3 minutes, or until soft. Add the garlic, ginger, and spices. Cook, stirring, for 1 minute.

3. Add the lentils and 2 cups of water and bring to a boil. Lower the heat and simmer, stirring occasionally, for 15 minutes, or until all the water has been absorbed.

4. Transfer to a serving bowl and serve warm with pita bread.

guacamole

SERVES 4 TO 6

2 avocados

½ small red onion, finely chopped

1 tomato, seeded and chopped

1 tablespoon lemon juice

3 tablespoons sour cream

1. Cut the avocados in half and remove the pits.

2. Peel the avocados and place the flesh into a bowl. Mash with a fork until smooth.

3. Add the onion, tomato, lemon juice, and sour cream. Stir to combine. Serve as a dip with pita bread, corn chips, or nachos.

nachos

SERVES 6 TO 8

15 1/2 ounces canned red kidney beans

3 tablespoons oil

1 large onion, peeled and chopped

2 garlic cloves, crushed

2 large ripe tomatoes, seeded and chopped

1/2 cup tomato salsa

hot pepper sauce

26 ounces corn chips

2 1/2 cups grated Cheddar cheese

guacamole (see page 21) and sour cream, to serve

1 Preheat the oven to 350°F. Rinse the kidney beans in a colander and drain. Mash with a fork.

2 Heat the oil in a skillet over medium heat and cook the onion and garlic until soft.

3 Add the tomatoes, tomato salsa, and mashed kidney beans, and cook until the tomatoes are soft. Season to taste with the hot pepper sauce.

4 Arrange half the corn chips in a flat ovenproof baking dish. Top with half the kidney bean mixture and then 1 cup of the grated cheese.

5 Repeat with the remaining ingredients to make a second layer. Bake in the oven for 10 to 15 minutes, or until the cheese has melted and the nachos are heated through. Serve the nachos topped with guacamole and sour cream.

sticky chicken drumsticks

SERVES 4

2 tablespoons honey

2 tablespoons sweet chile sauce

2 tablespoons ketchup

2 tablespoons dark soy sauce

2 tablespoons light soy sauce

3½ pounds skinless chicken drumsticks

2 tablespoons sesame seeds

1 Put the honey, chile sauce, ketchup, and soy sauces in a large nonreactive dish and stir together. Cut 2 to 3 slits across each drumstick with a knife.

2 Coat the drumsticks in the marinade. Cover and refrigerate for at least 2 hours, or overnight. Turn in the marinade 2 to 3 times.

3 Preheat the oven to 350°F. Line a large baking sheet with waxed paper. Sprinkle the sesame seeds over the chicken and put them on the sheet.

4 Bake for 45 minutes, or until cooked and golden, turning and brushing with the marinade 2 to 3 times. Serve warm or cold.

fresh spring rolls

MAKES 8

½ rotisserie chicken

1¾ ounces dried rice vermicelli

8 (6½-inch) square dried rice paper wrappers

16 basil leaves

1 large handful cilantro leaves

1 carrot, cut into short, thin strips and blanched

2 tablespoons Chinese plum sauce

1 Remove the meat from the chicken, discard the skin, and finely shred the meat. Soak the vermicelli in hot water for 10 minutes and then drain.

2 Dip a rice paper wrapper into warm water for 10 to 15 seconds, or until it softens, then place it on a clean work surface. Put one-eighth of the chicken on the wrapper and top with two basil leaves, a few cilantro leaves, a few carrot strips, and a small amount of vermicelli. Spoon a little sauce over the top.

3 Press the filling down to flatten it a little, then fold in one side and roll it up tightly like a parcel. Lay the roll, seam side down, on a serving plate and sprinkle with a little water. Cover with a damp cloth and repeat with the remaining ingredients. Serve with your favorite dipping sauce or a little extra plum sauce.

cream of tomato soup

SERVES 4

1 tablespoon olive oil

1 onion, finely chopped

2 garlic cloves, crushed

3 (14-ounce) cans crushed tomatoes

3 cups chicken stock

1 tablespoon tomato paste

2 teaspoons light brown sugar

1 cup half-and-half

1 Heat the oil in a large saucepan. Add the onion and cook until soft and lightly golden, stirring occasionally. Add the garlic and cook for 1 more minute.

2 Add the tomatoes, stock, tomato paste, and sugar to the saucepan. Bring to a boil, then reduce the heat.

3 Simmer the soup, partially covered with a lid, for 20 minutes. Let the soup cool a little, then process in batches in a blender or food processor until smooth.

4 Return the soup to the pan, stir in the half-and-half, and reheat gently. Don't let the soup boil once you have added the half-and-half, or it will curdle.

pumpkin soup

SERVES 4 TO 6

2¼ pounds butternut squash

4 tablespoons butter

1 onion, chopped

4 cups chicken stock

¾ cup half-and-half

1 Cut the squash into large pieces, then cut off all the skin. Chop into smaller pieces. This is best done by an adult.

2 Heat the butter in a large saucepan. Add the onion and cook gently for 15 minutes, or until very soft.

3 Add the squash and stock to the pan. Cover with a lid and bring to a boil, then reduce the heat and simmer for 20 minutes, or until the squash is tender.

4 Let the soup cool a little, then process in batches in a blender or food processor until smooth.

5 Return the soup to the pan and add the half-and-half and salt and pepper to taste. Stir over low heat until heated through. Don't let the soup boil once you have added the half-and-half, or it will curdle.

chicken noodle omelet

SERVES 2

3-ounce packet chicken-flavored
instant noodles

1 cup chopped cooked chicken

2 teaspoons finely chopped Italian parsley

2 eggs, lightly beaten

2 tablespoons grated Cheddar cheese

1 Boil 2 cups of water in a saucepan. Add the noodles and their flavor packet to the saucepan. Cook the noodles as directed. Drain well.

2 Put the noodles, chicken, parsley, and eggs in a bowl. Mix well.

3 Put the mixture in a 8-inch nonstick ovenproof skillet. Cook for 5 minutes without stirring.

4 Sprinkle with the cheese. Put under a broiler and broil for 2 minutes, or until browned. Serve hot.

corn fritters

SERVES 4

1 large red bell pepper

2 to 3 cobs fresh corn or
1½ cups canned corn kernels, drained

oil, for frying

2 tablespoons chopped Italian parsley,
cilantro leaves, chives, or dill

3 eggs

1 Cut the pepper into large pieces, discarding the seeds and membrane, then chop into small pieces. If using fresh corn, cut the kernels from the cob, using a sharp knife.

2 Heat 2 tablespoons of oil in a skillet. Add the corn and pepper and stir for 2 minutes. Transfer the vegetables to a bowl. Add the herbs and stir well to combine. Beat the eggs in a small bowl with a little pepper. Stir the egg gradually into the vegetable mixture.

3 Heat a nonstick skillet over medium heat. Add enough oil to just cover the base. Drop large spoonfuls of the vegetable mixture into the pan, a few at a time. Cook the fritters for 1 to 2 minutes, or until browned. Turn over and cook the other side. Drain on paper towels and keep warm while you cook the remainder.

strawberry shake

SERVES 2

1 cup chopped strawberries (or raspberries)

1 cup whole milk

3 scoops vanilla or strawberry ice cream

sugar, if using raspberries

1 Put the strawberries or raspberries (and sugar, to taste), milk, and ice cream into a blender and blend until smooth.

2 Pour into two cups and serve.

banana smoothie

SERVES 2

1 banana, roughly chopped

1 tablespoon plain yogurt

1 teaspoon honey

1 cup whole milk

1 Put the banana in a blender with the yogurt, honey, and milk and blend until smooth, thick, and creamy.

2 Pour into two cups and serve.

berry froth

SERVES 2

1 2/3 cups fresh or frozen mixed berries

2 cups whole milk

2 ice cubes

sugar

1 Put the mixed berries, milk, and ice cubes in a blender and blend until smooth. Add the sugar to taste and blend again until combined.

2 Pour into two large cups and serve.

fresh fruit slushy

SERVES 4

½ cup chopped fresh pineapple

1 banana, cut into chunks

3 kiwi fruit, sliced

1 cup tropical-blend fruit juice

2 ice cubes

1 Put the pineapple and banana in a blender with the kiwi fruit, fruit juice, and ice cubes and blend until smooth.

2 Pour into four cups and serve.

malted milkshake

SERVES 2

1 cup whole milk

1 tablespoon chocolate drink powder

1 tablespoon powdered malt

4 scoops vanilla ice cream

1 Combine the milk, chocolate powder, malt, and ice cream in a blender and blend for 1 minute.

2 Pour into two glasses and serve.

mango whiz

SERVES 1

$1/2$ cup ice cubes

$1^1/_2$ cups chopped fresh mango

1 Put the ice cubes in a blender and blend until roughly chopped.

2 Add the mango and blend until the fruit and ice are well mixed.

3 Pour into a glass and serve. Add a little water or orange juice to make the drink a little thinner if you like.

peach dream

SERVES 4

15 ounces canned peach slices, drained

2 cups vanilla ice cream

3 tablespoons orange juice

2 to 3 drops vanilla extract

2 cups chilled whole milk

1 Combine the peach slices, vanilla ice cream, orange juice, vanilla extract, and chilled milk in a blender and blend until smooth.

2 Pour into four glasses and serve.

moo juice

SERVES 8

$1^3/_4$ cups (14 ounces) fruit-flavored yogurt

2 tablespoons honey

1 teaspoon vanilla extract

2 ripe bananas

2 cups chilled whole milk

4 scoops vanilla ice cream

1 Combine the yogurt, honey, vanilla extract, bananas, milk, and ice cream in a blender and blend for 3 minutes.

2 Divide among eight glasses and serve.

dinnertime

pizza

SERVES 4

1 large fresh or frozen prebaked
pizza shell

tomato sauce

1 tablespoon olive oil

1 small onion, chopped

1 garlic clove, crushed

1 large tomato, seeded and chopped

1 tablespoon tomato paste

½ teaspoon dried oregano

napolitana topping

grated mozzarella cheese, chopped dried
oregano, sliced pitted black olives, and
thinly sliced anchovy fillets (optional)

pepperoni topping

red pepper, pepperoni and
grated mozzarella cheese

1 To make the tomato sauce, heat the olive oil in a small
saucepan over medium heat and add the onion and
garlic. Cook for 3 minutes, or until soft.

2 Add the chopped tomato and stir to combine.
Reduce the heat to low and simmer for 10 minutes,
stirring occasionally.

3 Stir in the tomato paste and oregano, and simmer for
another 2 minutes. Set aside to cool.

4 Preheat the oven to 425°F. Put the pizza shell on a
nonstick pizza sheet or a large baking sheet lined
with waxed paper. Spread the tomato sauce over the
pizza shell.

5 Top with your favorite topping to make either a
napolitana or pepperoni pizza. Bake for 30 minutes.

fettuccine carbonara

SERVES 4

2 teaspoons oil

8 slices uncooked bacon, cut into thin strips

1 pound fettuccine

4 eggs

1/2 cup grated Parmesan cheese

1 cup whipping cream

1 Heat the oil in a skillet and cook the bacon over medium heat until brown and crisp. Remove from the skillet and drain on paper towels.

2 Add the fettuccine to a large saucepan of boiling water and cook until just tender. Drain well in a colander, then return to the pan.

3 Put the eggs, cheese, and cream into a small bowl and beat together with a fork. Add the bacon.

4 Pour the sauce over the hot pasta. Stir over very low heat for 1 minute, or until the sauce thickens.

quick pasta with tomato sauce

SERVES 4

1 tablespoon extra-virgin olive oil

1 garlic clove, crushed

1 3/4 cups (14 ounces) canned chopped tomatoes

1 pound penne

1 tablespoon grated Parmesan cheese

1 Heat the olive oil in a skillet over medium heat. Cook the garlic, stirring constantly, for 30 seconds. Add the tomatoes and stir through. Reduce the heat to low and cook for a further 8 to 10 minutes, stirring occasionally, or until reduced.

2 Meanwhile, cook the pasta in a large saucepan of boiling water until just tender. Drain and return to the saucepan.

3 Add the cooked tomatoes to the pasta and stir through. Spoon into bowls and sprinkle with Parmesan cheese.

spaghetti bolognese

SERVES 4

1 teaspoon olive oil

1 large onion, finely chopped

3 garlic cloves, crushed

1 celery stalk, diced

1 carrot, diced

1 pound lean ground beef

1 tablespoon dried oregano

2 cups beef stock

2 tablespoons tomato paste

3½ cups (28 ounces) canned chopped tomatoes

1 pound spaghetti

1 Heat the oil in a nonstick saucepan over medium heat. Add the onion and cook for 2 to 3 minutes, or until softened. Add the garlic, celery, and carrot and cook for 2 to 3 minutes, or until softened.

2 Add the beef and cook over high heat for 5 minutes, or until browned, breaking up any lumps with the back of a spoon.

3 Add the oregano and 1 cup of water, and cook for 3 to 4 minutes, or until almost all the liquid has evaporated. Add the stock, tomato paste, and tomatoes, and season with salt and pepper.

4 Reduce the heat to low and simmer, covered, for 1½ hours, stirring occasionally to prevent the sauce from sticking to the bottom. If the sauce is too thin, remove the lid and simmer until it has reduced and thickened.

5 Cook the pasta in a large saucepan of boiling water for 10 minutes, or until tender. Drain and toss with the bolognese sauce.

lasagne

SERVES 6

1 tablespoon olive oil

1 large onion, finely chopped

3 large garlic cloves, crushed

1 celery stalk, diced

1 carrot, diced

3/4 cup sliced button mushrooms

1 pound lean ground beef

1 teaspoon drled oregano

2 cups beef stock

2 tablespoons tomato paste

3 1/2 cups (28 ounces) canned
chopped tomatoes

1 pound Swiss chard

1 1/2 tablespoons butter

4 tablespoons all-purpose flour

1 1/2 cups whole milk

2/3 cup ricotta cheese

13 ounces oven-ready lasagna sheets
(about 12 large sheets)

2/3 cup grated Cheddar cheese

1. Heat the oil in a large saucepan over high heat. Add the onion and cook for 2 minutes. Add the garlic, celery, carrot, and mushrooms, and cook for 2 minutes. Add the beef and cook for 5 minutes, or until cooked. Add the oregano and cook for 3 to 4 minutes.

2. Add 1 cup of water, the stock, tomato paste, and tomatoes and season. Reduce the heat to low and simmer, covered, for 1 1/2 hours, stirring occasionally. Cool slightly. Wilt the washed chard for 1 minute in a covered pan.

3. To make the white sauce, melt the butter in a saucepan over medium heat. Stir in the flour and cook for 1 minute. Slowly stir in the milk, and keep stirring until the sauce boils and thickens. Simmer for 2 minutes. Stir in the ricotta until smooth.

4. Preheat the oven to 400°F. Arrange a third of the pasta over the bottom of a large ovenproof baking dish. Spread with half the beef, then half the spinach. Make another layer of pasta and spread with the remaining beef, then the spinach, then the remaining pasta. Top with the white sauce, sprinkle with Cheddar cheese, and bake for 30 minutes, or until golden.

spaghetti with chicken meatballs

SERVES 4

tomato sauce

1 teaspoon olive oil

2 garlic cloves, crushed

3½ cups (28 ounces) canned crushed tomatoes

chicken meatballs

1 pound ground chicken

2 garlic cloves, crushed

¼ cup fresh bread crumbs

2 tablespoons chopped fresh basil

¼ teaspoon cayenne

1 tablespoon olive oil

2 tablespoons chopped fresh basil

1 pound spaghetti

2 tablespoons grated Parmesan cheese

1   To make the tomato sauce, heat the oil in a large nonstick saucepan over medium heat. Add the garlic and cook for 1 minute, or until just turning golden. Add the tomatoes and season. Lower the heat and simmer for 15 minutes, or until thickened.

2   Line a baking sheet with waxed paper. To make the meatballs, combine the chicken, garlic, bread crumbs, basil, and cayenne in a large bowl and season.

3   Using damp hands, roll tablespoons of the mixture into balls and place on the baking sheet.

4   Heat the olive oil in a skillet over medium heat. Cook the meatballs in batches, turning, for 3 to 4 minutes, or until golden. Transfer the meatballs to the sauce and simmer for a further 10 minutes, or until cooked through. Add the basil.

5   Meanwhile, cook the spaghetti in a large saucepan of boiling water for 10 minutes, or until tender. Drain well. Toss the spaghetti with the meatballs and sauce and serve with the grated Parmesan cheese.

san choy bau

SERVES 4

3 tablespoons Chinese oyster sauce

2 teaspoons soy sauce

3 tablespoons Chinese rice wine

1 teaspoon sugar

1½ tablespoons vegetable oil

¼ teaspoon sesame oil

3 garlic cloves, crushed

3 teaspoons grated fresh ginger

6 scallions, sliced on the diagonal

1 pound ground pork

½ cup finely chopped bamboo shoots

½ cup finely chopped water chestnuts

1 tablespoon pine nuts, toasted

12 small or 4 large whole lettuce leaves (such as iceberg)

Chinese oyster sauce, to serve

1   To make the sauce, combine the oyster and soy sauces, rice wine, and sugar in a small bowl and stir until the sugar dissolves.

2   Heat a wok over high heat, pour in the vegetable and sesame oils, and swirl to coat the wok. Add the garlic, ginger and half the scallion and stir-fry for 1 minute. Add the pork and cook for 3 to 4 minutes, or until just cooked, breaking up any lumps.

3   Add the bamboo shoots, water chestnuts, and remaining scallion, then pour in the sauce. Cook for 2 to 3 minutes, or until the liquid thickens a little. Stir in the pine nuts.

4   Trim the lettuce leaves into cup shapes. Divide the filling among the lettuce cups to make either twelve small portions or four very large ones. Drizzle with oyster sauce, then serve.

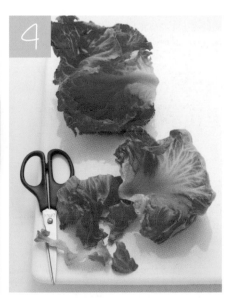

orange and ginger chicken stir-fry

SERVES 4 TO 6

3 tablespoons vegetable oil

4 to 6 boneless, skinless chicken thighs, cut into small pieces

3 teaspoons grated fresh ginger

1 teaspoon grated orange zest

1/2 cup chicken stock

2 teaspoons honey

1 1/4 pounds bok choy, trimmed and halved lengthwise

toasted sesame seeds, to serve

steamed white rice, to serve

1 Heat a wok over high heat, pour in the oil, and swirl to coat the side of the wok. Add the chicken in batches and stir-fry each batch for 3 to 4 minutes, or until golden.

2 Return all the chicken to the wok, add the ginger and orange zest, and cook for 20 seconds, or until fragrant.

3 Add the stock and the honey, and stir to combine. Increase the heat and cook for 3 to 4 minutes, or until the sauce has thickened slightly.

4 Add the bok choy and cook until slightly wilted. Season well, then sprinkle with toasted sesame seeds and serve with steamed rice.

sweet chile chicken and noodles

SERVES 4

12 ounces egg noodles

4 boneless, skinless chicken thighs, cut into small pieces

1 to 2 tablespoons sweet chile sauce

2 teaspoons Asian fish sauce

1 tablespoon vegetable oil

3½ ounces baby sweet corn, halved lengthwise

5½ ounces snow peas, trimmed

1 tablespoon lime juice

1 Put the noodles in a large bowl, cover with boiling water for 1 minute, then gently separate. Drain and rinse.

2 Combine the chicken, sweet chile sauce, and fish sauce in a bowl.

3 Heat a wok over high heat, pour in the oil, and swirl to coat the side of the wok. Add the chicken and stir-fry for 3 to 5 minutes, or until cooked through. Add the corn and snow peas, and stir-fry for 2 minutes. Stir in the noodles and lime juice, then serve.

pork, squash, and cashew stir-fry

SERVES 4

2 to 3 tablespoons vegetable oil

½ cup cashews

1⅔ pounds pork loin fillet

1 pound winter squash, cut into cubes

1 tablespoon grated fresh ginger

4 tablespoons chicken stock

3 tablespoons Chinese rice wine

1½ tablespoons soy sauce

½ teaspoon cornstarch

¾ pound bok choy

1 to 2 tablespoons cilantro leaves

1   Heat a wok over high heat, pour in 1 tablespoon of the oil, and swirl to coat the wok. Stir-fry the cashews for 1 to 2 minutes, or until browned. Remove and drain on a paper towel.

2   Slice the pork thinly across the grain. Reheat the wok, add a little extra oil, and swirl to coat. Stir-fry the pork in batches for 5 minutes, or until lightly browned. Remove. Add 1 tablespoon of oil and stir-fry the squash and ginger for 3 minutes, or until lightly browned. Add the stock, rice wine, and soy sauce, and simmer for 3 minutes, or until the squash is tender.

3   Blend the cornstarch with 1 teaspoon of water, add to the wok, and stir until the mixture boils and thickens. Return the pork and cashews to the wok, and add the bok choy and cilantro. Stir until the bok choy has just wilted. Serve with steamed rice.

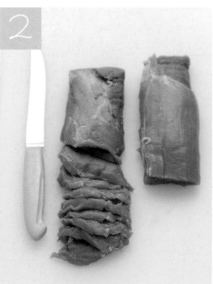

spinach and ricotta cannelloni

SERVES 4

1 tablespoon unsalted butter

1 small onion, finely chopped

2 garlic cloves, crushed

3 bunches Swiss chard

1¼ cups ricotta cheese

1 tablespoon dried oregano

tomato sauce

1 tablespoon olive oil

1 small onion, finely chopped

2 garlic cloves, crushed

2 cups (15½ ounces) canned tomatoes

½ cup tomato pasta sauce

1 teaspoon dried oregano

2 teaspoons Dijon mustard

1 tablespoon balsamic vinegar

1 teaspoon sugar

12 oven-ready lasagna noodles

½ cup grated mozzarella cheese

½ cup grated Parmesan cheese

1. Preheat the oven to 350°F. To make the filling, melt the butter in a saucepan and cook the onion and garlic for 3 to 5 minutes, until softened. Shred the chard, add to the pan, and cook for 5 minutes, or until wilted and the moisture has evaporated. Remove from the heat and leave to cool. Put in a blender with the ricotta and oregano, and process until smooth.

2. To make the sauce, heat the oil in a saucepan and cook the onion and garlic over low heat for 5 minutes. Add the rest of the sauce ingredients. Bring to a boil, then simmer for 10 minutes, or until thick.

3. Cut the lasagna into twelve 4½-inch squares. Lightly grease a large ovenproof baking dish and spread a third of the sauce over the base.

4. Spoon chard filling down the side of each lasagna square, then roll up the pasta around the filling and put, seam side down, in the dish. Space out the cannelloni evenly, then spread the remaining sauce over the top. Sprinkle with mozzarella and Parmesan, and bake for 30 to 35 minutes, or until golden.

pea and ham risotto

1 tablespoon olive oil

1 celery stalk, chopped

2 tablespoons chopped Italian parsley

1/2 cup (2 1/2 ounces) chopped sliced ham

1 2/3 cups peas, fresh or frozen

3 cups chicken stock

4 tablespoons unsalted butter

1 onion, chopped

2 cups Arborio rice

1/3 cup grated Parmesan cheese, plus extra to serve

1 Heat the oil in a skillet and add the celery and parsley. Cook over medium heat for a few minutes. Add the ham and stir for 1 minute. Add the peas and 3 tablespoons of water and bring to a boil, then reduce the heat and simmer, uncovered, until almost all the liquid has evaporated. Set aside. Put the stock and 3 cups of water in a saucepan and keep at simmering point.

2 Heat the butter in a saucepan. Add the onion and stir until softened. Add the rice and stir well. Pour in 3 tablespoons of water. Add 1/2 cup of stock to the rice mixture. Stir over low heat until the stock has been absorbed. Repeat until all the stock has been added and the rice is creamy and tender.

3 Add the pea mixture and Parmesan and serve with the extra Parmesan.

chicken and leek risotto

4 tablespoons unsalted butter

1 leek, thinly sliced

2 boneless, skinless chicken breasts, finely chopped

2 cups Arborio rice

5 cups chicken stock

1/3 cup grated Parmesan cheese

1 Preheat the oven to 300°F. Heat the butter in an ovenproof baking dish with a lid over medium heat. Add the leek and cook for 2 minutes, or until softened but not browned.

2 Add the chicken and cook, stirring, for 2 to 3 minutes, or until it is golden on both sides. Add the rice and stir so that it is well coated with butter. Cook for 1 minute.

3 Add the stock and 3 tablespoons of water, and bring to a boil. Cover and bake in the oven for 30 minutes, stirring halfway through cooking time. Remove from the oven and stir through the Parmesan. Season.

pork and chive dumplings

MAKES 24

1 teaspoon vegetable oil

2 garlic cloves, crushed

1 teaspoon finely grated fresh ginger

2 teaspoons snipped chives

1/2 carrot, finely diced

7 ounces ground pork

2 tablespoons Chinese oyster sauce

3 teaspoons salt-reduced soy sauce,
plus extra to serve

1/2 teaspoon sesame oil

1 teaspoon cornstarch

24 round gyoza skins

1 Heat a wok over high heat, pour in the vegetable oil, and swirl to coat the side of the wok. Add the garlic, ginger, chives, and carrot, then stir-fry for 2 minutes. Remove the wok from the heat.

2 Put the pork, oyster sauce, soy sauce, sesame oil, and cornstarch in a bowl and mix well. Add the vegetable mixture once it has cooled, mixing it into the pork mixture.

3 Put 2 teaspoons of the mixture in the center of each gyoza skin. Moisten the edges with water, then fold in half to form a semicircle. Pinch the edges together to form a ruffled edge.

4 Line a double bamboo steamer with waxed paper. Put half the dumplings in a single layer in each steamer basket. Cover and steam over a wok of simmering water for 12 minutes, or until cooked through. Serve with soy sauce.

sausage pie

SERVES 4

3 thick or 6 thin, fresh Italian sausages

4 sheets frozen puff pastry, thawed

4 eggs

1 Put the sausages in a large bowl and cover with boiling water. Leave until cool. When cool, carefully peel the skins from the sausages and slice.

2 Use half the pastry to line a 10-inch pie dish or four individual baking dishes. Arrange the sausages evenly in the dish. Beat the eggs and season with salt and pepper, then gently pour over the sausages.

3 Preheat the oven to 375°F. Use the rest of the pastry to cover the pie, trim the excess, and seal the edges well. Cut two small slits in the middle. Cut out star shapes and place on top, if desired. Brush with some beaten egg.

4 Bake for 45 minutes. Serve hot or cold.

burger with the works

SERVES 4

burgers

1 pound lean ground beef

1 onion, finely chopped

1 egg, lightly beaten

1/3 cup fresh bread crumbs

2 tablespoons ketchup

2 teaspoons Worcestershire sauce

toppings

2 tablespoons butter

2 large onions, cut into rings

4 Cheddar cheese slices

4 slices uncooked bacon

4 eggs

4 large hamburger buns, halved

1 handful lettuce leaves

1 large tomato, sliced

4 pineapple rings

ketchup, to serve

1 Place all the burger ingredients in a mixing bowl. Use your hands to mix together until well combined.

2 Divide the mixture into 4 portions and shape each portion into a patty.

3 Melt the butter in a skillet and cook the onion until soft. Set aside and keep warm.

4 Cook the burgers in the skillet for 4 minutes each side. Place a slice of cheese on each burger, to melt.

5 Cook the bacon in the skillet (without any butter) until crisp, then fry the eggs.

6 Toast the buns under a broiler for 3 to 5 minutes and place the bottom of the buns on serving plates. On each bun, place the lettuce, tomato, and pineapple, then a burger. Follow with bacon, onion, egg, tomato sauce, and finally the top of the bun.

fried rice

2 tablespoons peanut oil

2 eggs, well beaten

4 slices uncooked bacon, chopped

2 teaspoons finely grated fresh ginger

1 garlic clove, crushed

6 scallions, finely chopped

1/3 cup seeded and diced red bell pepper

1 teaspoon sesame oil

4 cups cold, cooked long-grain white rice

2/3 cup frozen peas, thawed

1 cup chopped cooked chicken

2 tablespoons soy sauce

1 Heat a large heavy-bottomed wok until very hot. Pour in 2 teaspoons of the peanut oil and swirl to coat the wok. Pour in the eggs and swirl to coat a little up the side of the wok. Cook until just set into an omelet. Remove from the wok, roll up, and set aside.

2 Add the remaining peanut oil to the wok and stir-fry the bacon for 2 minutes. Add the ginger, garlic, scallion, and red pepper, and stir-fry for 2 minutes.

3 Add the sesame oil and the rice. Stir-fry, tossing regularly, until the rice is heated through.

4 Cut the omelet into thin strips and add to the wok with the peas and the chicken. Cover and steam for 1 minute, or until heated through. Stir in the soy sauce and serve.

potato gnocchi with tomato sauce

SERVES 4 TO 6

tomato sauce

1 tablespoon oil

1 onion, chopped

1 celery stalk, chopped

2 carrots, chopped

2 (14-ounce) cans crushed tomatoes

1 teaspoon sugar

potato gnocchi

2¼ pounds russet potatoes

2 tablespoons butter

2 cups all-purpose flour

2 eggs, beaten

2 tablespoons finely grated mozzarella cheese, to serve

1 To make the tomato sauce, heat the oil in a saucepan, add the onion, celery, and carrot, and cook for about 5 minutes, stirring. Add the tomatoes and sugar, and season. Bring to a boil, then reduce the heat to very low and simmer for 20 minutes. Cool a little, then process, in batches, in a food processor until smooth.

2 To make the potato gnocchi, peel the potatoes, chop roughly, and boil until very tender. Drain and mash until smooth. Using a wooden spoon, stir in the butter and flour, then beat in the eggs. Leave to cool.

3 Turn out the gnocchi mixture onto a floured surface and divide into four. Roll each into a sausage shape.

4 Cut into short pieces and press each piece with the back of a fork. Cook the gnocchi in batches in a large saucepan of boiling salted water for about 2 minutes, or until they rise to the surface. Using a slotted spoon, drain the gnocchi and transfer to bowls. Serve with the tomato sauce. Sprinkle with mozzarella cheese.

crisp-battered fish and wedges

SERVES 4

3 russet potatoes

oil, for deep-frying

1 cup self-rising flour

1 egg, beaten

¾ cup soda water

4 boneless firm white fish fillets
(such as grouper or catfish), cut into strips

all-purpose flour, for dusting

½ cup tartar sauce, or mayonnaise
mixed with 1 tablespoon lemon juice

1. Wash the potatoes, but do not peel. Cut into thick wedges, then dry with paper towels. Fill a heavy-bottomed saucepan two-thirds full with oil and heat. Gently lower the potato wedges into medium-hot oil. Cook for 4 minutes, or until tender and lightly browned. Carefully remove the wedges from the oil with a slotted spoon and drain on paper towels.

2. Sift the self-rising flour with some pepper into a large bowl and make a well in the center. Add the egg and soda water. Using a wooden spoon, stir until just combined and smooth. Dust the fish fillets in the all-purpose flour, shaking off the excess. Add the fish fillets one at a time to the batter and toss until well coated. Remove the fish from the batter, draining off the excess batter.

3. Working with one piece of fish at a time, gently lower it into the medium-hot oil. Cook for 2 minutes, or until golden and crisp and cooked through. Carefully remove from the oil with a slotted spoon. Drain on paper towels, and keep warm while you cook the remainder.

4. Return the potato wedges to the medium-hot oil. Cook for another 2 minutes, or until golden brown and crisp. Remove from the oil with a slotted spoon and drain on paper towels. Serve the wedges immediately with the fish, and tartar sauce or lemon mayonnaise.

Note: This recipe has ingredients that are deep-fried, so you'll need an adult to help you if you are cooking on your own.

fish cakes

1½ pounds russet potatoes, peeled and quartered

2 tablespoons canola oil

1 pound boneless white fish fillets (such as cod)

1 leek, white part only, finely chopped

2 garlic cloves, crushed

¼ cup chopped scallions

lemon wedges, to serve

1 Put the potato in a saucepan. Cover with cold water and bring to a boil. Boil for 15 minutes, or until the potato is tender. Drain well. Mash with a fork.

2 Meanwhile, heat 2 teaspoons of the oil in a large nonstick skillet over medium heat. Add the fish fillets and cook for 3 to 4 minutes on each side, or until cooked. Set aside to cool. Flake the fish with a fork.

3 Heat another 2 teaspoons of the oil in the same skillet over medium heat. Cook the leek and garlic, stirring often, for 5 to 6 minutes, or until the leek softens. Set aside on a plate.

4 Mix together the mashed potato, flaked fish, leek mixture, and scallion in a large bowl. Shape into eight cakes and put on a plate. Cover and refrigerate for 1 hour.

5 Heat the remaining oil in the skillet over medium heat. Cook the fish cakes for 3 to 4 minutes on each side, or until lightly golden.

tuna enchiladas

MAKES 8

1 tablespoon light olive oil

1 onion, thinly sliced

3 garlic cloves, crushed

2 teaspoons ground cumin

1/2 cup vegetable stock

15 ounces canned tuna in brine, drained

3 tomatoes, peeled, seeded, and chopped

1 tablespoon tomato paste

15 ounces canned three-bean mix

2 tablespoons chopped cilantro leaves

8 flour tortillas

1 small avocado, pitted and chopped

1/2 cup light sour cream

1 handful cilantro sprigs

2 cups shredded lettuce

1 Preheat the oven to 325°F. Heat the oil in a deep saucepan or a deep-frying pan on medium heat. Add the onion and cook for 3 to 4 minutes, or until just soft. Add the garlic and cook for another 30 seconds. Add the cumin, vegetable stock, tuna, tomato, and tomato paste, and cook for 6 to 8 minutes, or until the mixture is thick.

2 Drain and rinse the bean mix. Add the beans to the sauce and cook for 5 minutes to heat through, then add the chopped cilantro.

3 Meanwhile, wrap the tortillas in foil and warm in the oven for 3 to 4 minutes.

4 Place a tortilla on a plate and spread with a large scoop of the bean mixture. Top with some avocado, sour cream, cilantro sprigs, and lettuce. Roll up the enchiladas, tucking in the ends.

vegetarian chili

¾ cup bulgur

2 tablespoons olive oil

1 onion, finely chopped

2 garlic cloves, crushed

2 teaspoons ground cumin

1 teaspoon chile powder

½ teaspoon ground cinnamon

2 (14-ounce) cans crushed tomatoes

3 cups vegetable stock

15½ ounces canned red kidney beans,
rinsed and drained

15½ ounces canned chickpeas,
rinsed and drained

11 ounces canned corn kernels,
rinsed and drained

2 tablespoons tomato paste

plain yogurt, to serve

1 Put the bulgur in a heatproof bowl and pour in
1 cup of hot water. Leave to stand until needed.

2 Heat the oil in a large saucepan and add the onion.
Cook for about 10 minutes over medium heat, stirring
occasionally, or until soft and lightly golden. Add the
garlic, cumin, chile, and cinnamon, and stir-fry for
1 minute.

3 Add the bulgur and all the remaining ingredients,
except the yogurt, and stir to combine. Decrease the
heat to low and simmer for 30 minutes. Serve with a
dollop of yogurt.

bubble and squeak

SERVES 4 TO 6

²/₃ cup cubed russet potatoes, cooked

²/₃ cup cubed squash, cooked

1 cup grated cabbage, cooked

²/₃ cup small broccoli florets, cooked

4 eggs, beaten

2 chives, snipped

1 tablespoon unsalted butter

1   Put the vegetables in a bowl and mix well with the egg and chives.

2   Melt the butter in a large skillet and add the vegetable mixture. Cook over medium heat until the underside is golden, then cut into quarters and turn over. Cook the mixture for a little longer, until it is golden and the egg has set.

Note: "Bubble and Squeak" is a traditional English breakfast dish of leftover cabbage and potatoes, usually from a roast dinner the night before.

tofu with greens and noodles

SERVES 4

marinade

3 tablespoons oyster sauce

3 tablespoons hoisin sauce

2 tablespoons soy sauce

1½ tablespoons light brown sugar

3 teaspoons grated fresh ginger

3 garlic cloves, crushed

10½ ounces firm tofu, drained and cut into small cubes

10½ ounces dried thin egg noodles

1 teaspoon canola oil

4 red Asian shallots, thinly sliced

1 small red bell pepper, seeded and thinly sliced

7 ounces sugar snap peas, trimmed

14 ounces broccoli, cut into 2-inch lengths

½ cup vegetable stock or water

1 Combine the marinade ingredients in a plastic bowl. Add the tofu and gently stir through. Cover and refrigerate for at least 30 minutes.

2 Cook the noodles according to the directions and drain. Cut the noodles into short lengths with scissors.

3 Heat the oil in a large wok. Place the shallots and red pepper in the wok and stir-fry for 2 minutes, or until slightly softened. Add the peas, broccoli, and stock. Cover and cook for 2 to 3 minutes, or until the vegetables are just tender, stirring occasionally.

4 Add the tofu with the marinade and the noodles. Gently combine and stir until heated through. Serve immediately.

leek and cheese frittata

SERVES 6

2 tablespoons olive oil

3 leeks, white part only, thinly sliced

2 zucchini, thinly sliced

1 garlic clove, crushed

5 eggs, lightly beaten

4 tablespoons grated Parmesan cheese

1/4 cup diced Swiss cheese

1 Heat 1 tablespoon of the olive oil in a small ovenproof skillet. Add the leek and cook, stirring, over low heat until slightly softened. Cover and cook the leek for 10 minutes, stirring occasionally. Add the zucchini and garlic, and cook for another 10 minutes. Transfer the mixture to a bowl. Allow to cool, then season with pepper. Add the egg and cheeses and stir through.

2 Heat the remaining oil in the skillet, then add the egg mixture and smooth the surface. Cook over low heat for 15 minutes, or until the frittata is almost set.

3 Put the skillet under a broiler for 3 to 5 minutes, or until the top is set and golden. Allow the frittata to stand for 5 minutes before cutting into wedges and serving. Serve with a fresh green salad.

eat your greens

asparagus with parmesan

SERVES 2 TO 4

5 1/2 ounces asparagus spears

olive oil, for drizzling

grated Parmesan cheese, to serve

1 Gently bend the base of each asparagus spear to snap off the woody end. Discard the ends.

2 Put the asparagus in a large skillet and pour in enough hot water to just cover them. Put a lid on the pan and cook the asparagus for 2 minutes, or until they are bright green and tender-crisp. Drain well.

3 Serve drizzled with a little olive oil and sprinkled with freshly grated Parmesan cheese.

caesar salad

SERVES 4

4 slices white or sourdough bread, crusts removed and cut into cubes

3 slices uncooked bacon

1 head romaine lettuce

½ cup Parmesan cheese shavings

dressing

4 anchovies, chopped

1 egg yolk

2 tablespoons lemon juice

1 garlic clove, crushed

½ cup olive oil

1 Preheat the oven to 375°F. Spread the bread cubes on a baking sheet and bake for 10 minutes, or until golden.

2 Fry the bacon slices in a skillet over medium heat until crisp. Drain on paper towels. Put the lettuce leaves in a salad bowl with the bread cubes, bacon, and Parmesan.

3 To make the dressing, put the anchovies, egg yolk, lemon, juice, and garlic in a blender. Blend for 20 seconds, or until smooth. Add the oil in a thin, steady stream until the dressing is creamy. Drizzle over the salad.

mixed salad

SERVES 4

1 head romaine lettuce

3½ ounces arugula

1 small red bell pepper

9 ounces cherry tomatoes,
cut into wedges

1 small cucumber, thinly sliced

2 to 3 tablespoons snipped chives

vinaigrette

3 tablespoons olive oil

2 to 3 tablespoons white vinegar
or lemon juice

1 teaspoon sugar

1. Tear the lettuce and arugula into pieces and put in a large serving bowl.

2. Cut the red pepper in half lengthwise and remove the seeds and white membrane. Cut into thin strips.

3. Combine the red pepper, tomato, cucumber, and chives in the bowl with the lettuce and arugula.

4. To make the vinaigrette, whisk the oil, vinegar, and sugar in a small bowl. Season with some salt and pepper. Pour the vinaigrette over the salad just before serving.

greek salad

SERVES 4

1 green bell pepper

1 cup feta cheese

2 large or 3 small vine-ripened tomatoes,
cut into wedges

1 small cucumber, sliced

1 small red onion, thinly sliced (optional)

⅓ cup kalamata olives

2 to 3 tablespoons lemon juice

3 to 4 tablespoons olive oil

1. Cut the green pepper in half lengthwise and remove the seeds and white membrane. Cut the flesh into small squares.

2. Cut the feta cheese into small cubes.

3. Combine the green pepper, cheese, tomato, cucumber, onion, and olives in a large bowl. Drizzle with the lemon juice and oil. Sprinkle with salt and pepper. Toss gently to combine, then serve.

hash browns

SERVES 4

2 russet potatoes

oil, for frying

1 Fill a saucepan with water and bring to a boil. Peel the potatoes and cut them in half.

2 Put the potatoes into the saucepan. Bring the water back to a boil, then boil the potatoes for 10 minutes, or until just tender when pierced with a knife.

3 Drain the potatoes and leave until cool enough to handle. Grate the potatoes, put in a bowl, and season with salt and pepper. Mix through.

4 Shape the grated potato roughly into patties about 4 inches in diameter.

5 Heat enough oil to cover the bottom of a skillet and cook the patties for a few minutes on each side, or until golden brown and crispy. Drain on paper towels.

ratatouille

SERVES 6

2 tablespoons olive oil

1 large onion, chopped

2 garlic cloves, crushed

3 slender eggplants

3 small zucchini

1 green bell pepper

1 red bell pepper

3 large tomatoes, seeded and chopped

1 large handful basil, chopped

1 Heat the oil in a large saucepan and add the onion. Cook over medium heat for 10 minutes, or until browned. Add the garlic and cook for 1 more minute.

2 Meanwhile, slice the eggplants and zucchini fairly thickly.

3 Remove the seeds and white membranes from the peppers and cut into small squares.

4 Add all the vegetables to the pan. Cook, stirring frequently, for about 5 minutes. Reduce the heat to low, cover the pan with a lid, and cook for 15 minutes, stirring occasionally. Uncover the pan, increase the heat, and cook for another 5 minutes. Stir in the basil.

potato salad

SERVES 4

1¼ pounds all-purpose potatoes

½ small red onion, finely chopped

2 to 3 celery stalks, finely chopped

1 small green bell pepper, chopped

2 tablespoons finely chopped
Italian parsley

dressing

¾ cup mayonnaise

1 to 2 tablespoons white vinegar or
lemon juice

2 tablespoons sour cream

1 Wash and peel the potatoes. Cut into small pieces.
Cook the potato in a large saucepan of boiling water
for about 5 minutes, or until just tender. Drain the
potato and allow it to cool.

2 Combine the onion, celery, green pepper, and parsley
in a large bowl. Add the cooled potato.

3 To make the dressing, mix together the mayonnaise,
vinegar or juice, and sour cream. Season with salt
and pepper.

4 Pour the dressing over the potato and gently toss
to combine.

scalloped potatoes

SERVES 4

1 pound russet potatoes

⅔ cup whole milk

½ cup whipping cream

½ cup grated Cheddar cheese

1 tablespoon butter

1 Preheat the oven to 350°F. Brush an 8-inch shallow
ovenproof baking dish with melted butter or oil.

2 Peel the potatoes and cut into thin slices. Layer the
slices in the dish, overlapping them slightly.

3 Combine the milk and the cream, and drizzle over
the potato.

4 Sprinkle the cheese evenly over the potato, then dot
with the butter. Bake for 45 minutes, or until the
potato is tender and the top is golden brown.

stir-fried chinese vegetables

SERVES 4

10½ ounces baby bok choy

3½ ounces green beans

2 scallions

5½ ounces broccoli

1 red pepper

2 tablespoons oil

2 garlic cloves, crushed

2 teaspoons grated fresh ginger

1 tablespoon sesame oil

2 teaspoons soy sauce

1   Wash the bok choy and trim away the thick stalks. Cut the leaves into wide strips.

2   Cut the beans into 2-inch lengths and slice the scallions diagonally. Cut the broccoli into small florets and the red pepper into strips.

3   Heat the oil in a large skillet or wok. Put in the garlic and ginger, and cook over medium heat for 30 seconds, stirring constantly.

4   Add the beans, scallions, and broccoli and stir-fry for 3 minutes. Add the red pepper and stir-fry for 2 more minutes, then add the bok choy and stir for 1 more minute. Stir in the sesame oil and soy sauce, and toss through. Serve immediately.

honey carrots

SERVES 4

2 carrots

2 tablespoons butter

1 tablespoon honey

1   Peel the carrots and cut into thin slices. Steam or boil the carrots for about 3 minutes, or until tender. Drain well and return to the pan.

2   Add the butter and honey, and toss over medium heat until the butter has melted and the carrot is coated.

cauliflower in cheese sauce

SERVES 4

1 pound cauliflower, cut into florets

2 tablespoons butter

3 teaspoons all-purpose flour

3/4 cup whole milk

1/2 cup grated Cheddar cheese

1/3 cup fresh bread crumbs

1 Steam or microwave the cauliflower for a few minutes until just tender. Arrange the cooked cauliflower in a shallow, ovenproof baking dish.

2 Melt the butter in a small saucepan. Add the flour and cook, stirring, for 1 minute, or until golden.

3 Add the milk a little at a time, stirring until completely smooth between each addition.

4 When all the milk has been added, keep stirring over medium heat until the sauce boils and thickens. Simmer for 1 minute, still stirring.

5 Remove the pan from the heat and add almost all the cheese, reserving a couple of tablespoons. Stir until the cheese has melted.

6 Pour the sauce over the cauliflower. Sprinkle with the remaining cheese combined with the bread crumbs.

7 Place under a broiler for a few minutes, until the cheese on top has melted and the bread crumbs are golden brown.

stuffed peppers

SERVES 4

4 small red bell peppers

½ cup short-grain white rice

1 tablespoon olive oil

1 onion, finely chopped

2 garlic cloves, crushed

1 tomato, seeded and chopped

1 cup finely grated Cheddar cheese

¼ cup finely grated Parmesan cheese

1 handful basil, chopped

1 handful Italian parsley, chopped

1 Preheat the oven to 350°F. Cut the tops off the peppers and scoop out the seeds and white membranes.

2 Cook the rice in a large saucepan of boiling water until tender. Drain well and set aside to cool.

3 Heat the oil in a skillet and cook the onion for a few minutes until lightly golden. Add the garlic and cook for 1 more minute.

4 Add the onion and garlic to the rice, along with all the remaining ingredients. Mix everything together well and season with salt and pepper.

5 Spoon the rice filling into the red peppers and place on a baking sheet. Bake for 30 minutes, or until the red peppers are soft and the filling is brown on top.

stuffed mushrooms

SERVES 4 TO 6

8 large flat or 12 button mushrooms

2 tablespoons oil

1 small onion, finely chopped

4 slices uncooked bacon, chopped

1 cup fresh bread crumbs

1 tablespoon chopped Italian parsley

⅔ cup grated Parmesan cheese

1 Preheat the oven to 350°F. Brush a baking sheet with melted butter or oil.

2 Remove the stems of the mushrooms. Finely chop the stems.

3 Heat the oil in a skillet, add the onion and bacon, and cook until the bacon is lightly browned. Add the chopped mushroom stems and cook for 1 minute.

4 Transfer the mixture to a bowl. Add the bread crumbs, parsley, and Parmesan and stir to combine.

5 Place the mushroom caps onto the baking sheet and spoon the filling into the caps. Bake for 20 minutes, or until the mushrooms are tender and the topping is golden. Serve immediately.

sticky treats

pear and raspberry crumble

SERVES 6

6 large pears

2 tablespoons sugar

3 star anise (optional)

1 cup raspberries

1 cup all-purpose flour

1/2 cup light brown sugar

2/3 cup unsalted butter, cut into cubes

ice cream, to serve

1 Preheat the oven to 375°F. Peel, quarter, and core the pears, then cut each piece in half lengthwise. Put into a large saucepan and sprinkle with the sugar. Add 1 tablespoon of water and the star anise. Cover and bring to a boil.

2 Cook, covered, over medium–low heat for 10 minutes, stirring occasionally, until the fruit is tender but still holds its shape. Drain the pears and discard the star anise. Transfer to a large ovenproof baking dish or six 1-cup ramekins. Sprinkle the raspberries over the pears.

3 Combine the flour, sugar, and butter in a bowl. Use your fingertips to rub the butter into the flour, until the mixture resembles coarse bread crumbs. Sprinkle over the fruit, then bake for 20 to 25 minutes, until golden brown. Leave for 5 minutes, then serve with ice cream.

pavlova

SERVES 6 TO 8

4 egg whites

½ teaspoon cream of tartar

1 cup superfine sugar

2 tablespoons confectioners' sugar

1½ cups whipping cream

banana, raspberries, and blueberries,
to serve

pulp from 2 passion fruit, to decorate

1   Preheat the oven to 300°F. Line a baking sheet with waxed paper. Draw an 8-inch circle on the paper.

2   Using electric beaters, beat the egg whites in a large, dry bowl until soft peaks form. Add the cream of tartar. Gradually add the superfine sugar, beating well after each addition. Continue beating until the mixture is thick and glossy and the sugar has completely dissolved. Add the confectioners' sugar and beat.

3   To test if the sugar has dissolved, rub a small amount of the mixture between your thumb and forefinger. The mixture should feel just slightly gritty. If it feels very gritty, continue beating for a few more minutes.

4   Spread the meringue mixture onto the sheet, inside the marked circle. Bake for 40 minutes.

5   Whip the cream until soft peaks form. Slice the banana. Decorate the pavlova with cream and the fresh fruit. Spoon the passion fruit pulp over the top and serve immediately.

baked apples

SERVES 4

4 cooking apples

⅓ cup light brown sugar

1½ tablespoons chopped raisins

½ teaspoon ground cinnamon (optional)

1½ tablespoons unsalted butter

yogurt or whipping cream, to serve

1 Preheat the oven to 425°F. Core the apples and score the skin around the middle.

2 Combine the sugar, raisins, and cinnamon in a bowl.

3 Place each apple on a piece of foil and stuff it with the filling. Spread a little butter over the top of each apple, then wrap the foil securely around the apples to enclose them.

4 Bake for about 35 minutes, or until cooked. Serve with yogurt or cream.

bread and butter pudding

SERVES 4

butter, for greasing

6 slices bread

3 cups whole milk

¼ teaspoon grated lemon zest

½ cup sugar

4 eggs

⅔ cup dried mixed fruits (golden raisins, raisins, chopped dried apricots, currants, mixed candied citrus peel)

1 Preheat the oven to 350°F. Grease a large ovenproof baking dish or four small baking dishes. Butter the bread and cut off the crusts.

2 Heat the milk in a saucepan and add the lemon zest. Bring to a boil, then cover and remove from the heat, leaving the milk to infuse for 10 minutes. Beat the sugar and eggs together, then strain the milk over the eggs and mix well.

3 Scatter half the dried fruit over the bottom of the dish and arrange half the bread, buttered sides down, on top. Pour in half the custard, then repeat with the remaining fruit, bread, and custard.

4 Put the ovenproof baking dish (or small dishes) in a large roasting pan. Pour water into the pan to come halfway up the side of the dish (this is called a bain-marie). Bake for 35 minutes.

fruit jelly

MAKES 6

1 tablespoon gelatin powder

1½ cups unsweetened fruit juice

¾ cup pureed fresh or drained, canned fruit in natural juice

1 Sprinkle the gelatin over ½ cup of cool water in a small saucepan. Heat through, then add the fruit juice and heat again.

2 Pour into a mixing bowl and leave until it begins to thicken. Stir in the puréed fruit until well combined.

3 Transfer to six small dishes or glasses and refrigerate until set.

chocolate-honeycomb mousse

SERVES 4

2/3 cup whipping cream

10 1/2 ounces good-quality semisweet or milk chocolate, chopped

3 eggs, separated

2 chocolate-covered honeycomb bars or 2 chocolate bars, crumbled (see note)

1 Pour the cream into a heavy-bottomed saucepan over medium heat. Remove from the heat just before the cream begins to boil.

2 Add the chopped chocolate, stirring until the chocolate has melted and the mixture is well combined. Pour into a large mixing bowl and set aside to cool for a few minutes.

3 Using electric beaters, beat the egg yolks into the chocolate mixture and continue beating for 1 to 2 minutes, or until the mixture has thickened.

4 Put the egg whites into a clean bowl and whisk until stiff peaks form. Gently fold into the chocolate mixture with a large, flat metal spoon. Spoon into four 1/2-cup ramekins and refrigerate overnight to set. Serve with the honeycomb bars or grated chocolate on top.

Note: As chocolate-covered honeycomb bars are not available in the United States, use milk chocolate bars.

lemon cheesecakes

MAKES 12

9 ounces graham crackers

1½ teaspoons allspice

½ cup unsalted butter, melted

filling

1½ cups (13 ounces) cream cheese

1 tablespoon grated lemon zest

2 teaspoons vanilla extract

14 ounces canned sweetened
condensed milk

4 tablespoons lemon juice

1   Grease 12 standard muffin cups with melted butter or oil. Line each cup with two strips of waxed paper.

2   Put the cookies in a food processor and process until finely crushed. Add the allspice and melted butter, and process to combine.

3   Press half the crumb mixture into the bottoms of the muffin cups. Press the remainder around the sides of the cups. Use a flat-bottomed glass to press the crumbs firmly into place. Put in the fridge.

4   To make the filling, beat the cream cheese with electric beaters until smooth and creamy. Add the lemon zest and vanilla extract. Mix well. Gradually beat in the condensed milk and lemon juice. Beat for 5 minutes, or until the mixture is smooth.

5   Pour the filling into the crumb shells and smooth the tops. Refrigerate the cheesecakes overnight. Lift out of the muffin cups, using the waxed paper handles.

jam upside-down cakes

SERVES 6

½ cup strawberry jam

4 tablespoons unsalted butter

½ cup superfine sugar

1 egg

1¾ cups all-purpose flour

1 teaspoon baking powder

½ cup whole milk

1 Grease six individual ovenproof custard cups or a 4-cup ovenproof bowl with butter. Spread the jam in the bottom.

2 Beat the butter, sugar, and egg until smooth and creamy. Sift in the flour and baking powder. Add the milk and mix well. Spread the batter carefully on top of the jam in the ovenproof bowls.

3 Make a foil lid for each bowl. Press around the edges to seal tight. Make string handles for the bowls.

4 Put the bowls into a large saucepan. Pour enough hot water into the pan to come a third of the way up the bowls. Put the lid on the pan and place over low heat. Simmer for 1 hour. Keep refilling with water.

5 Run a knife around the edge of each cake. Unmold onto a serving plate, then serve.

lemon delicious

SERVES 4

4 tablespoons unsalted butter

3/4 cup sugar

3 eggs, separated

1 teaspoon grated lemon zest

1/3 cup self-rising flour

3/4 cup whole milk

3 tablespoons lemon juice

1 Preheat the oven to 350°F. Lightly grease a 4-cup ovenproof baking dish or four individual custard cups with a little melted butter.

2 Beat the butter, sugar, egg yolks, and lemon zest in a large bowl until the mixture is light and creamy. Fold in the flour, milk, and lemon juice.

3 Beat the egg whites in a bowl until soft peaks form. Fold into the butter and sugar mixture, then pour into the dish. Bake for 30 to 40 minutes, or until golden.

tangy lime delicious

SERVES 4

2 tablespoons butter

1 cup sugar

1 tablespoon grated lime zest

2 eggs, separated

1/3 cup self-rising flour

2/3 cup low-fat milk

1/2 cup lime juice

1 Preheat the oven to 350°F. Lightly grease a 4-cup ovenproof baking dish or four individual custard cups with a little melted butter.

2 Beat the butter, sugar, and lime zest in a bowl until the mixture is light and creamy. Gradually add the egg yolks, beating well between each addition.

3 Fold in the flour, milk, and lime juice. Beat the egg whites in a bowl until soft peaks form. Fold into the butter and sugar mixture, then pour into the baking dish. Bake for 30 to 40 minutes, or until golden.

crepes

MAKES ABOUT 12

1 cup all-purpose flour

sprinkle of salt

1 egg

1¼ cups whole milk

lemon juice and sugar, to sprinkle

whipped cream or ice cream, to serve

1 Sift the flour and salt into a mixing bowl and make a well in the center.

2 Add the egg and milk. Whisk until smooth. Set aside for 1 hour.

3 Gently heat a lightly greased 8-inch skillet. Pour about 3 tablespoons of batter into the pan. Tilt the pan to spread the batter evenly.

4 Lift the edges with a knife. When golden, flip the crepe over and cook the other side.

5 Sprinkle lemon juice and sugar over the crepe. Roll up and serve hot with whipped cream or ice cream.

sticky date cakes

SERVES 6

½ cup shredded dried coconut

½ cup light brown sugar

¾ cup self-rising flour

¼ cup all-purpose flour

½ teaspoon baking soda

⅔ cup unsalted butter

¼ cup light corn syrup or honey

1 cup chopped dates

3 tablespoons orange juice

2 eggs, lightly beaten

sauce

⅓ cup unsalted butter

¼ cup light brown sugar

1 cup whipping cream

2 tablespoons light corn syrup or honey

1 Preheat the oven to 350°F. Brush six small ovenproof bowls with melted butter or oil.

2 Combine 2 tablespoons each of the coconut and brown sugar and sprinkle into the bowls.

3 Sift the flours and soda into a mixing bowl. Add the remaining coconut and make a well in the center.

4 Combine the remaining sugar, butter, corn syrup, dates, and orange juice in a saucepan. Stir over medium heat until the butter melts.

5 Using a metal spoon, fold the date mixture into the dry ingredients. Add the eggs and stir until smooth.

6 Pour the batter into the bowls and bake for 35 minutes. Leave the cakes in the bowls for 5 minutes before unmolding.

7 To make the sauce, combine all the ingredients in a saucepan. Stir over low heat until the sugar and butter have dissolved. Stir for a further 2 minutes, then serve over the hot cake.

upside-down banana cake

SERVES 6

½ cup unsalted butter

¾ cup granulated sugar

1 egg

2 cups all-purpose flour

2 teaspoons baking powder

¾ cup whole milk

1 large banana, mashed

⅓ cup unsalted butter, melted

½ cup light brown sugar

1 cup canned crushed pineapple, drained

whipped cream, to serve

1 Preheat the oven to 350°F. Grease six small springform cake pans or an 8-inch springform cake pan.

2 Beat the butter, sugar, and egg until smooth. Sift in the flour and baking powder. Mix well, then add the milk and mashed banana.

3 Spread the melted butter in the base of each tin, then sprinkle evenly with the brown sugar.

4 Spread the crushed pineapple over the sugar. Pour the batter evenly over the top. Bake for 40 to 45 minutes.

5 Unmold onto a plate. Serve warm with cream.

caramel sauce

SERVES 6 TO 8

$^2/_3$ cup unsalted butter

1 cup light brown sugar

$^1/_2$ cup whipping cream

1 Combine all the ingredients in a small saucepan. Stir over medium heat until the mixture is smooth. Bring to a boil, reduce the heat slightly, and simmer for 2 minutes.

strawberry sauce

SERVES 8

9 ounces strawberries

2 tablespoons superfine sugar

1 tablespoon orange or lemon juice

1 Put the strawberries, sugar, and juice into a blender and blend until the mixture is smooth. Chill in the refrigerator.

hot chocolate sauce

SERVES 6 TO 8

9 ounces semisweet chocolate

$^2/_3$ cup whipping cream

2 tablespoons light corn syrup or honey

$2^1/_2$ tablespoons unsalted butter

1 Chop the chocolate roughly. Place the chocolate, cream, corn syrup, and butter in a saucepan. Stir over low heat until the chocolate has melted and the mixture is smooth. Serve immediately.

banana split

SERVES 4

4 large ripe bananas, halved lengthwise

8 small scoops vanilla ice cream

sauce of your choice

mixed candies, to decorate

12 small white or pink marshmallows

$^1/_4$ cup crushed nuts

1 Arrange the two halves of each banana in a long, shallow serving dish and top with two scoops of ice cream.

2 Pour over the sauce of your choice. Decorate with the candies, marshmallows, and crushed nuts and serve immediately.

cookies, cakes, and sweets

chocolate brownies

MAKES ABOUT 30

⅓ cup all-purpose flour

½ cup unsweetened cocoa powder

2 cups sugar

1 cup chopped pecans or pistachios

9 ounces semisweet chocolate, chopped

1 cup unsalted butter, melted

2 teaspoons vanilla extract

4 eggs, lightly beaten

1 Preheat the oven to 350°F. Grease and line a 9 x 13-inch rectangular cake pan. Sift the flour and cocoa into a large bowl, add the sugar and nuts, and mix well. Stir in the chocolate and make a well in the center.

2 Add the butter, vanilla, and eggs. Stir until combined.

3 Pour the mixture into the pan and smooth the surface. Bake for 45 minutes. Cool in the pan before cutting into squares.

chocolate chip cookies

MAKES ABOUT 22

1½ cups all-purpose flour

1 cup unsweetened cocoa powder

1½ cups light brown sugar

¾ cup unsalted butter

5½ ounces semisweet chocolate, chopped

3 eggs, lightly beaten

1 cup semisweet chocolate chips

⅓ cup white chocolate chips

5½ ounces nuts of your choice, chopped (such as macadamias, pecans, almonds, brazils, walnuts, or pistachios)

1 Preheat the oven to 350°F. Line two baking sheets with waxed paper.

2 Sift the flour and cocoa into a bowl and stir in the sugar. Make a well in the center.

3 Heat the butter and chocolate in a saucepan over low heat. Stir until the mixture is smooth.

4 Stir the butter mixture and eggs into the dry ingredients. Mix until well combined. Stir in the dark and white chocolate chips and the nuts.

5 Drop heaping tablespoons of the mixture onto the sheets. Flatten each one slightly with your fingertips.

6 Bake for 15 minutes. Leave on the sheets for at least 5 minutes before transferring to a wire rack to cool.

gingerbread people

MAKES ABOUT 16

½ cup unsalted butter

½ cup light brown sugar

⅓ cup light corn syrup or honey

1 egg

2 cups all-purpose flour

⅓ cup self-rising flour

1 tablespoon ground ginger

1 teaspoon baking soda

frosting

1 egg white

½ teaspoon lemon juice

1 cup confectioners' sugar

assorted food colorings

1 Line two baking sheets with waxed paper. Beat the butter, sugar, and corn syrup in a bowl until light and creamy. Add the egg and beat well. Sift in the flours, ginger, and baking soda. Use a knife to mix until combined.

2 Divide the dough into two balls. Knead on a floured surface until smooth. Roll out the dough between two sheets of waxed paper to a ¼-inch thickness. Refrigerate for 30 minutes. Preheat the oven to 350°F.

3 Cut the dough into people, using cutters. Press any remaining dough together. Reroll and cut out into shapes. Bake for 10 minutes, or until browned. Once cool, decorate with the frosting.

4 To make the frosting, beat the egg white in a bowl with electric beaters until soft peaks form. Add the lemon juice and confectioners' sugar, and beat until thick and creamy.

5 Divide the frosting into bowls and tint with the food colorings. Spoon into piping bags and use to decorate the cookies.

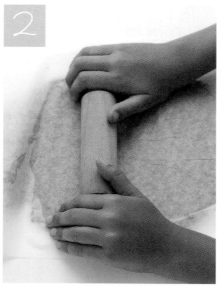

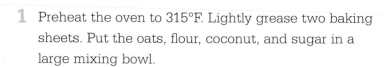

anzac cookies

MAKES ABOUT 25

2 cups rolled oats

1 cup all-purpose flour

2 cups shredded dried coconut

1½ cups sugar

1 cup unsalted butter

4 tablespoons light corn syrup or honey

1 teaspoon baking soda

1 Preheat the oven to 315°F. Lightly grease two baking sheets. Put the oats, flour, coconut, and sugar in a large mixing bowl.

2 Melt the butter and corn syrup in a saucepan, stirring. Remove from the heat.

3 Mix the baking soda and 2 tablespoons of boiling water in a cup. Add to the melted butter in the saucepan. Add to the bowl and mix well to combine.

4 Roll tablespoons of the mixture into balls. Put on sheets spacing them 2 inches apart. Press lightly with a fork. Bake for 20 minutes, one sheet at a time, until golden and crisp.

melting moments

MAKES ABOUT 45

⅓ cup cornstarch

1 cup all-purpose flour

¾ cup unsalted butter

⅓ cup confectioners' sugar

1 teaspoon vanilla extract

½ cup candied cherries, halved

1 Preheat the oven to 350°F. Line two baking sheets with waxed paper.

2 Sift the cornstarch and flour into a bowl.

3 Put the butter, sugar, and vanilla into a mixing bowl and beat with electric beaters until light and creamy.

4 Using a flat-bladed knife, stir the cornstarch and flour into the butter mixture until just combined and the mixture is smooth.

5 Spoon teaspoons of the mixture onto the baking sheets, leaving room for spreading.

6 Top each cookie with half a cherry and bake for 15 minutes, or until lightly golden and crisp.

7 Transfer the cookies to a wire rack to cool.

muesli bars

MAKES 18 BARS

1 cup unsalted butter

1 cup sugar

2 tablespoons honey

2¹/₂ cups rolled oats

³/₄ cup shredded dried coconut

1 cup cornflakes, lightly crushed

¹/₂ cup flaked almonds

1 teaspoon pumpkin pie spice

¹/₂ cup finely chopped dried apricots

1 cup all-purpose flour

1 cup dried mixed fruit

1 Preheat the oven to 315°F. Brush a shallow 8-inch square cake pan with melted butter or oil. Line with waxed paper.

2 Put the butter, sugar, and honey in a small saucepan and stir over low heat until the butter has melted and the sugar has dissolved.

3 Put the oats, coconut, cornflakes, almonds, spice, apricots, flour, and mixed fruit into a large mixing bowl and mix until well combined. Make a well in the center.

4 Add the butter and sugar mixture, and mix until well combined. Put into the cake pan.

5 Bake for 30 to 45 minutes, or until golden. Using a sharp knife, cut lines to divide the cake up into 18 pieces but do not cut right through to the bottom. Leave in the pan for 15 minutes before turning it out onto a board to cool. Cut fully into bars when cold.

caramel bars

MAKES 18 TO 20 BARS

½ cup all-purpose flour

½ cup self-rising flour

1 cup shredded dried coconut

⅔ cup unsalted butter

½ cup light brown sugar

filling

2 tablespoons unsalted butter

2 tablespoons light corn syrup or honey

14 ounces sweetened condensed milk

topping

5½ ounces semisweet chocolate,
roughly chopped

2½ tablespoons unsalted butter

1 Preheat the oven to 350°F. Line a shallow 7 x 11-inch baking pan with waxed paper. Sift the flours together into a bowl. Stir in the coconut and make a well in the center.

2 Combine the butter and sugar in a saucepan and stir over low heat until the butter has melted. Pour into the dry ingredients and stir well to combine.

3 Press the mixture evenly into the pan with the back of a spoon. Bake for 10 minutes, then leave to cool.

4 To make the filling, combine the butter, corn syrup, and condensed milk in a saucepan. Stir over low heat until smooth. Continue stirring for 10 minutes. Pour over the pastry base and bake for 20 minutes.

5 To make the topping, place the chocolate and butter in a heatproof bowl over a saucepan of barely simmering water. Stir until smooth.

6 Spread over the caramel and leave to set. Lift from the pan and cut into bars or squares to serve.

jam thumbprints

MAKES ABOUT 32

¹/₃ cup unsalted butter

¹/₃ cup sugar

2 tablespoons whole milk

¹/₂ teaspoon vanilla extract

1 cup self-rising flour

¹/₃ cup instant vanilla pudding mix

2 tablespoons strawberry jam

1 Preheat the oven to 350°F. Line two baking sheets with waxed paper.

2 Using electric beaters, beat the butter and sugar in a small bowl until the mixture is light and creamy. Add the milk and vanilla, and beat until combined.

3 Sift the flour and pudding mix into the butter mixture and mix to form a soft dough.

4 Roll 2 teaspoons of the dough at a time into balls and place on the baking sheets.

5 Press a hollow in each ball with your thumb or the end of a wooden spoon and fill each hole with ¹/₄ teaspoon of jam.

6 Bake the cookies for 15 minutes, then transfer to a wire rack to cool.

rocky road

MAKES ABOUT 36 PIECES

¼ cup shredded dried coconut

3½ ounces white marshmallows

3½ ounces pink marshmallows

⅓ cup unsalted mixed nuts

¼ cup candied cherries, halved

13 ounces semisweet chocolate chips

1 Line a shallow 7 x 11-inch cake pan with foil. Sprinkle half the coconut over the bottom of the pan.

2 Cut the marshmallows in half and arrange in the pan, alternating colors and leaving a little space between the pieces. Sprinkle the remaining coconut, nuts, and cherries in the spaces between the marshmallows and around the edge of the pan.

3 Place the chocolate in a heatproof bowl. Put the bowl over a saucepan of simmering water and stir until the chocolate has melted. Cool slightly. Pour over the marshmallow mixture.

4 Tap the cake pan gently on the bench to settle the chocolate. Leave to set. When firm, cut into pieces with a sharp knife.

coconut ice

MAKES 30 PIECES

- 2½ cups confectioners' sugar
- ¼ teaspoon cream of tartar
- 1 egg white, lightly beaten
- 3 tablespoons unsweetened condensed milk
- 1¾ cups shredded dried coconut
- pink food coloring

1 Brush a 13¾-inch loaf pan with melted butter or oil. Line with waxed paper and grease the paper. Sift the confectioners' sugar and cream of tartar into a bowl. Make a well in the center.

2 Add the combined egg white and condensed milk. Stir in the coconut. Mix until well combined. Divide the mixture between two bowls. Tint the contents of one bowl with pink coloring. Knead the color through evenly.

3 Press the pink mixture into the bottom of the loaf pan. Cover with the white mixture and press down gently. Refrigerate for 1 hour, or until set.

4 When firm, remove from the pan and cut into squares.

chocolate cake

SERVES 8 TO 10

½ cup unsalted butter

¾ cup sugar

3 eggs

1 tablespoon light corn syrup or honey

1 teaspoon vanilla extract

1½ cups all-purpose flour

½ teaspoon baking powder

¼ tablespoon baking soda

3 tablespoons unsweetened cocoa powder

½ cup whole milk

frosting

1 cup confectioners' sugar

1½ tablespoons unsweetened cocoa powder

1½ tablespoons unsalted butter, softened

1 Preheat the oven to 350°F. Grease an 8-inch springform cake pan. Line with waxed paper. Beat the butter, sugar, and eggs until smooth and creamy.

2 Stir in the corn syrup and vanilla. Sift in the flour, baking powder, baking soda, and cocoa. Mix in the milk.

3 Spread evenly in the cake pan. Bake for 45 to 55 minutes.

4 Leave to stand for 10 minutes, then remove from the pan. Cool completely.

5 To make the frosting, mix the confectioners' sugar, cocoa, and butter with a little hot water. When smooth, spread over the cake.

Scones

MAKES 12

2 cups self-rising flour

pinch of salt

2 tablespoons unsalted butter

$3/4$ cup whole milk or buttermilk

extra milk, for glazing

butter or jam and whipped cream, to serve

1 Preheat the oven to 425°F. Brush a baking sheet with melted butter or oil.

2 Sift the flour and salt into a large bowl. Add the butter and rub it in lightly using your fingertips, until it looks like fine bread crumbs.

3 Make a well in the center. Add almost all the milk and mix with a spatula to a soft dough, adding more milk if necessary.

4 Turn out the dough onto a lightly floured surface and knead briefly until smooth. Roll out the dough to $1/2$ to $3/4$ inch thick. Cut into twelve rounds with a 2-inch cutter.

5 Place the rounds close together on the baking sheet. Brush the tops with a little extra milk. Bake for 10 to 15 minutes, or until golden brown. Serve with butter, or jam and whipped cream.

meringues

MAKES 35

3 egg whites

1/2 cup superfine sugar

1/3 cup confectioners' sugar

1/2 tablespoon cream of tartar

1 Preheat the oven to 300°F. Line a baking sheet with waxed paper.

2 Beat the egg whites until stiff. Gradually blend in the superfine sugar until thick and glossy.

3 Fold in the icing sugar and cream of tartar. Spoon or pipe small mounds onto the baking sheet.

4 Reduce the oven temperature to 200°F. Bake for 45 to 55 minutes, or until dry.

carrot cake with ricotta topping

SERVES 12 TO 14

2¹/₂ cups self-rising flour

1 teaspoon baking soda

2 teaspoons ground cinnamon

1 teaspoon pumpkin pie spice

¹/₂ cup light brown sugar

¹/₂ cup golden raisins

2 eggs, lightly beaten

2 tablespoons canola oil

4 tablespoons milk

¹/₂ cup apple puree

10¹/₂ ounces carrots, coarsely grated

ricotta topping

¹/₂ cup ricotta cheese

¹/₄ cup confectioners' sugar

1 teaspoon grated lime zest

1 Preheat the oven to 350°F. Lightly grease an 8 x 4-inch loaf pan and line the bottom with waxed paper. Sift the flour, baking soda, and spices into a large bowl. Stir in the brown sugar and raisins.

2 Combine the eggs, oil, milk, and apple puree. Stir the egg mixture into the flour mixture.

3 Add the carrots and mix well to combine. Spread into the loaf pan and bake for 1 hour 15 minutes, or until the cake comes away slightly from the sides. Leave for 5 minutes, then turn out onto a wire rack.

4 To make the topping, beat the ricotta, confectioners' sugar, and lime zest together until smooth. Spread over the cooled cake.

cupcakes

MAKES ABOUT 18

2 cups self-rising flour

3/4 cup sugar

1/2 cup unsalted butter, softened

3 eggs

3 tablespoons milk

1/2 teaspoon vanilla extract

frosting

3/4 cup confectioners' sugar

1 teaspoon unsweetened cocoa powder

1 1/2 tablespoons unsalted butter, softened

chocolate disks, to decorate

1. Preheat the oven to 350°F. Line 18 standard muffin cups with paper liners.

2. Sift the flour and sugar into a mixing bowl. Add the butter, eggs, milk, and vanilla, and beat until smooth. Fill the paper liners three-quarters full with the batter.

3. Bake for 15 minutes, or until the cupcakes are golden. Cool on a wire rack.

4. To make the frosting, mix the confectioners' sugar, cocoa, and butter with a little hot water until smooth. Spread over the cakes. Top each cake with a chocolate disk.

lemon butterfly cakes

MAKES 18

2 cups self-raising flour

3/4 cup sugar

1/2 cup unsalted butter, softened

3 eggs

3 tablespoons whole milk

1/2 teaspoon vanilla extract

2 teaspoons grated lemon zest

2/3 cup lemon buttercream frosting

1/2 cup whipping cream

18 silver dragées

1. Preheat the oven to 350°F. Line 18 standard muffin cups with paper liners.

2. Sift the flour and sugar into a bowl. Add the butter, eggs, milk, and vanilla, and beat until smooth. Mix in the zest. Fill the paper liners three-quarters full with the batter. Bake for 15 minutes, or until golden.

3. Cut a circle from the top of each cake. Cut the circles in half. Put 1/2 teaspoon of lemon buttercream frosting into each cake.

4. Beat the cream until firm peaks form. Put 1 tablespoon of cream onto each cake. Press the half-circles on top to form "wings." Decorate with silver dragées.

apple and orange mini cakes

MAKES 24

2/3 cup unsalted butter

2/3 cup light brown sugar

1 tablespoon honey

1 egg

1 cup apple puree

1 cup whole wheat self-rising flour

1/2 cup self-rising flour

1 teaspoon ground cinnamon

pinch of ground cloves

orange glaze frosting

1 cup confectioners' sugar

1/2 tablespoon unsalted butter

1 teaspoon grated orange zest

2 tablespoons orange juice

1 Preheat the oven to 350°F. Grease 24 mini muffin cups. Beat the butter, sugar, and honey together until light and creamy, then add the egg and apple puree and beat until well combined.

2 Sift in the flours and spices, and mix well. Spoon the batter into the muffin cups and bake for 20 minutes. Allow to cool.

3 To make the frosting, mix the confectioners' sugar, butter, orange zest, and orange juice in a heatproof bowl. Place over a saucepan of simmering water and stir until smooth. Allow to cool slightly, then top the cakes with frosting.

let's party

zebra sandwiches

MAKES 6

8 slices white bread

1½ tablespoons butter

4 tablespoons chocolate-hazelnut spread

1 Spread three slices of bread with butter and chocolate-hazelnut spread. Stack the slices, spread side up. Top with the unbuttered slice. Press down gently. Do the same with the other four slices of bread.

2 Remove the crusts with a sharp knife and cut each stack into three fingers.

banana and date fingers

MAKES 18

1½ tablespoons butter

12 slices white bread

3 bananas, mashed

6 fresh dates, chopped

1 Butter the bread and spread six slices with mashed banana and top with dates. Top with the remaining six slices of bread to make sandwiches.

2 Remove the crusts with a sharp knife and cut each sandwich into three fingers.

mini burgers

MAKES 10 SMALL OR 20 MINI

1 pound ground beef

1 small onion, finely chopped

1 tablespoon finely chopped Italian parsley

1 egg, lightly beaten

1 tablespoon ketchup

2 tablespoons oil

1/2 lettuce, finely shredded

2 small tomatoes, thinly sliced

10 small bread rolls or 20 mini dinner rolls, cut in half

2 3/4 ounces Cheddar cheese, thinly sliced

5 canned pineapple rings, drained and quartered

ketchup or barbecue sauce, to serve

1 Combine the beef, onion, parsley, beaten egg, and tomato sauce in a large bowl. Using your hands, mix until well combined.

2 Divide the mixture into ten portions or twenty smaller portions. Shape into round patties.

3 Heat the oil in a large, heavy-bottomed skillet over medium heat. Cook the patties for 5 minutes on each side, or until they are well browned and cooked through. Remove and drain on paper towels.

4 To assemble the burgers, put lettuce and tomato on the bottom of each roll. Top with a meat patty, cheese slice, and pineapple piece. Add the sauce and cover with the top of the roll. Serve immediately.

baked sweet potato wedges

SERVES 4

3 pounds sweet potatoes

2 tablespoons olive oil

1 Preheat the oven to 400°F. Peel and slice the sweet potatoes into wedges.

2 Put the wedges in a large baking tin and toss with the olive oil. Bake for about 30 minutes, or until browned and crisp. Serve warm.

baked chicken nuggets

SERVES 4

1¹/₃ cups cornflakes

14 ounces boneless, skinless chicken breasts

all-purpose flour, for dusting

1 egg white, lightly beaten

1 Preheat the oven to 400°F. Put the cornflakes in a food processor and process to fine crumbs.

2 Cut the chicken breasts into bite-size pieces. Toss in seasoned flour, then in the egg white. Roll each piece in the cornflake crumbs until well coated.

3 Lightly grease a baking sheet with oil and place the nuggets on it. Bake for 10 minutes, or until golden and cooked through.

cocktail bonbons

MAKES 12

12 small good-quality cocktail sausages

3 sheets frozen puff pastry, thawed

1 egg, lightly beaten

cotton or jute string

1 Preheat the oven to 350°F. Line two baking sheets with waxed paper.

2 Prick the sausages with a fork. Cut each pastry sheet into four squares. Brush each square with beaten egg.

3 Place a sausage on each pastry square and roll it up. Gently press the edges together.

4 Carefully pinch in the ends of the pastry. Tie the ends loosely with pieces of string.

5 Place the pastries on the baking sheets. Brush lightly with the beaten egg. Bake for 15 minutes, or until golden. Remind your party guests not to eat the string!

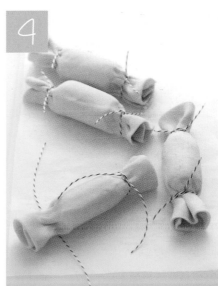

animal crisps

MAKES 20

1 sheet frozen puff pastry, thawed

1 egg, lightly beaten

¼ cup grated Cheddar cheese

1 Preheat the oven to 350°F. Line a baking sheet with waxed paper.

2 Cut animal shapes out of the pastry, using assorted cookie cutters. Place on the baking sheet.

3 Brush with the egg. Sprinkle the shapes with cheese. Bake for 10 to 15 minutes, or until golden and crisp.

caramel popcorn balls

MAKES 50

2 tablespoons oil

½ cup popping corn

¾ cup sugar

⅓ cup unsalted butter

2 tablespoons honey

2 tablespoons whipping cream

1 Heat the oil in a large saucepan over medium heat. Add the corn and cover with a lid. Cook for 5 minutes, or until the popping stops, shaking the pan occasionally. Turn out the popcorn into a big bowl.

2 Put the sugar, butter, honey, and cream in a small saucepan. Stir over medium heat, without boiling, until the sugar has completely dissolved. Bring to a boil and boil, without stirring, for 5 minutes.

3 Pour the caramel over the popcorn and mix together. Leave to cool a little, then rub some oil over your hands and mold the popcorn into small balls. Put on a wire rack to set.

baby chocolate éclairs

MAKES ABOUT 24

⅓ cup unsalted butter

1 cup all-purpose flour

4 eggs

4½ ounces semisweet
chocolate, melted

whipped cream, to serve

1 Preheat the oven to 400°F. Line a baking sheet with waxed paper. Put the butter in a saucepan and add 1 cup of water. Bring to a boil. Sift in all the flour. Cook, stirring, until the mixture forms a ball. Leave to cool for 5 minutes.

2 Add the eggs, one at a time, beating well until thick and glossy. Spoon into a piping bag and pipe short lengths onto the baking sheet. Sprinkle with a little water.

3 Bake for 10 to 15 minutes. Reduce the oven temperature to 350°F and bake for a further 10 to 15 minutes, or until golden and firm.

4 Pierce the side of each éclair with a skewer to allow steam to escape. Turn off the oven and return the éclairs to the oven for about 5 minutes to dry out. Cool on a wire rack.

5 Split the éclairs in half lengthwise and remove any uncooked pastry. Spread the tops with chocolate, leave to set, fill with cream, and replace the tops.

pecan tarts

MAKES 8

8 frozen shortcrust pastry shells

¹/₄ cup self-rising flour

¹/₂ teaspoon pumpkin pie spice

²/₃ cup chopped pecan nuts

1 egg, lightly beaten

1 tablespoon milk

2 tablespoons light corn syrup or honey

¹/₂ teaspoon vanilla extract

1 Preheat the oven to 375°F. Arrange the pastry cases on a baking sheet.

2 Sift the flour and spice into a bowl. Stir in the nuts. Make a well in the center.

3 Add the egg, milk, corn syrup, and vanilla. Beat with a fork until almost smooth.

4 Spoon the filling evenly into the pastry shells. Bake on the top rack of the oven for 15 minutes. Allow to cool on a wire rack.

beach baby jellies

MAKES 12

2 x 3 oz packets lime gelatin

2 tablespoons fine cookie crumbs

12 gummy candies

12 Lifesavers

12 paper parasols

1 Combine the lime gelatin and 2 cups of boiling water in a bowl. Stir until all the gelatin has dissolved. Set aside until cool. Pour the mixture into small molds to three-quarters full. Refrigerate overnight.

2 Sprinkle the cookie crumbs over half of each gelatin dessert. Lay a gummy candy on the crumbs. Place a Lifesaver on the crumbs and put a paper parasol through the center.

bleeding fingers

2 egg whites

1/2 cup sugar

1 cup shredded dried coconut

1/2 cup raspberry or strawberry jam

10 colored jelly beans

1 Preheat the oven to 300°F. Line a baking sheet with waxed paper.

2 Beat the egg whites until stiff peaks form. Beat in the sugar, 1 tablespoon at a time, and continue beating until the mixture becomes thick and glossy. Fold in the coconut.

3 Fill a piping bag fitted with a plain 3/4-inch nozzle with the meringue mixture. Pipe 31/4-inch lengths onto the baking sheet.

4 Bake for 5 minutes. Reduce the heat to 235°F and bake for a further 45 to 50 minutes, or until the meringues are light and crisp. Turn off the oven and leave the meringues inside to cool.

5 Heat the jam in a saucepan over low heat until thin and runny. Pour into a bowl. Cut one end from each jelly bean and discard the end. Cut the remaining jelly beans in half lengthwise. Press the jelly bean on the end of each meringue. Drizzle with warm jam to resemble the blood.

bloodbaths

MAKES 12

101/2 ounces frozen raspberries

3 sheets frozen puff pastry, thawed

1/4 cup confectioners' sugar, sifted

1 Place the raspberries in a bowl. Allow to stand for 10 to 15 minutes, or until thawed slightly. Refrigerate.

2 Preheat the oven to 350°F. Brush 12 standard muffin cups with melted butter or oil. Cut the sheets of pastry into four equal squares and line each muffin cup with the pastry.

3 Bake for 15 minutes, or until golden. Place on a wire rack to cool and allow the puff pastry to settle. Using the back of a spoon, carefully push down the center of the pastry to form a cup shape.

4 Combine the semifrozen raspberries and confectioners' sugar in a food processor and process until smooth. Pour the raspberry mixture into the cooled pastry shells.

milk chocolate banana bites

MAKES ABOUT 10

4¹/₂ ounces milk chocolate, chopped

1 teaspoon oil

2 bananas, peeled and cut into 1¹/₄-inch slices

¹/₂ cup chocolate jimmies

1 Melt the chocolate in a bowl over hot water. Take off the heat. Add the oil and stir until smooth.

2 Spread the sprinkles on baking waxed. Using a skewer, dip the banana into the chocolate, then roll in the jimmies. Put on waxed paper and leave to set. Serve on the skewers.

dark chocolate banana bites

MAKES 9

3 large bananas, peeled and cut into thirds

4¹/₂ ounces semisweet chocolate, chopped

1 Line a large baking sheet with foil. You need nine wooden Popsicle sticks. Push a stick into each piece of banana. Put on the sheet and freeze for 2 hours, or until firm.

2 Melt the chocolate in a bowl over hot water. Dip the banana pieces in the chocolate. Refrigerate until the chocolate has set, then wrap in plastic wrap and place in the freezer for at least 2 hours. Serve frozen.

frozen fruit kebabs

MAKES 4

5 ounces fresh pineapple

¹/₂ mango

2³/₄ ounces fresh watermelon, pits removed

3¹/₂ ounces fresh cantaloupe or any orange-fleshed melon

1 Remove the skin from all the fruit and cut into cubes or shapes.

2 You need four wooden Popsicle sticks. Thread pieces of fruit onto each stick and freeze for 4 hours, or until frozen.

3 Remove from the freezer 10 minutes before eating to allow them to soften slightly.

fruity frozen yogurt

MAKES 6

2 (7-ounce) containers vanilla-flavored yogurt

6 ounces canned passion fruit pulp in syrup

4 large strawberries, cut into small pieces

1 tablespoon confectioners' sugar

1 Put the yogurt, passion fruit, and strawberries in a bowl.

2 Add the confectioners' sugar and mix well.

3 Spoon into six glasses and freeze for 1 hour. Serve frozen.

squelch and crunch

MAKES 20

6½ ounces whole chocolate cookies

½ cup sugar

2 teaspoons gelatin powder

1 teaspoon vanilla extract

2 to 3 drops pink food coloring

colored dragées, to decorate

1   Line two baking sheets with foil. Place the cookies on the sheets.

2   Combine the sugar, gelatin, and ½ cup of water in a saucepan. Stir over medium heat until the sugar dissolves and the mixture comes to a boil. Simmer, without stirring, for 4 minutes. Remove from the heat and let cool.

3   Using an electric mixer, beat the syrup for 5 to 6 minutes, or until the mixture is thick and glossy.

4   Add the vanilla and coloring, and beat well. Spread a small amount to cover each cookie. Smooth the surface and sprinkle with colored dragées.

swamp mud

SERVES 8

5½ ounces semisweet chocolate, chopped

4 eggs, separated

2 tablespoons sugar

1 teaspoon grated orange zest

4 tablespoons whipping cream

1 teaspoon gelatin powder

1 tablespoon orange juice

jimmies, to decorate

1   Place the chocolate in a small heatproof bowl and sit it over a saucepan of simmering water. Stir until the chocolate has melted and the mixture is smooth. Cool slightly.

2   Using an electric mixer, beat the egg yolks, sugar, and zest in a large bowl for 5 minutes, or until thick and creamy. Beat in the cream and melted chocolate.

3   Combine the gelatin with the juice in a bowl. Stand the bowl in hot water and stir until the gelatin dissolves. Add to the chocolate mixture and beat until combined.

4   Place the egg whites in a clean, dry bowl. Using an electric mixer, beat until firm peaks form. Add to the chocolate mixture. Fold in together until well combined. Refrigerate for 2 hours, or until set. Decorate with jimmies.

chocolate chip crackles

MAKES 24

3 cups puffed rice cereal

1/4 cup unsweetened cocoa powder

1 1/4 cups confectioners' sugar

1/2 cup golden raisins

2/3 cup shredded dried coconut

7 ounces vegetable shortening, melted

1/3 cup semisweet chocolate chips

colored sprinkles, to decorate

1 Line 24 mini muffin cups with foil or doubled paper liners. Combine the puffed rice cereal, cocoa, and sugar in a large bowl. Mix thoroughly, then stir in the raisins and coconut. Stir in the melted shortening.

2 Spoon the mixture into the paper liners. Sprinkle with the chocolate chips and top with colored sprinkles. Refrigerate until set.

chocolate-cherry spiders

MAKES 20

½ cup candied cherries, finely chopped

⅓ cup flaked almonds, toasted

3½ ounces fried egg noodles

7 ounces semisweet chocolate, chopped

2 tablespoons unsalted butter

1 Put the cherries in a bowl with the flaked almonds and noodles.

2 Melt the chocolate and butter in a small heatproof bowl over hot water. Stir until smooth.

3 Add the chocolate to the cherry mixture and stir gently to combine.

4 Put spoonfuls of the mixture onto a sheet of waxed paper. Leave to set.

fairy wands

MAKES 10

½ cup unsalted butter, softened

½ cup sugar

1 egg

2 cups all-purpose flour

7 ounces semisweet chocolate chips, melted

10 Popsicle sticks

small dragées, to decorate

1 Beat the butter, sugar and egg with an electric mixer until creamy. Add the flour. Using your hands, press the mixture together to make a soft dough. Turn onto a lightly floured work surface and knead for 2 minutes, or until smooth. Cover with plastic wrap and put in the refrigerator for 30 minutes.

2 Preheat the oven to 350°F. Brush a large baking sheet with melted butter or oil. Roll out the dough between sheets of waxed paper to ¼ inch thick. Cut the dough into twenty stars, using a star-shaped cutter. Arrange on the baking sheets and bake for 15 minutes, or until golden. Cool on the trays.

3 Place ½ teaspoon of melted chocolate on the flat side of half the cookies. Spread out to cover.

4 Attach the stick and sandwich the remaining cookies over the chocolate and press together. Allow the chocolate to set.

5 Drizzle the remaining chocolate over the stars. Decorate with dragées and allow to set.

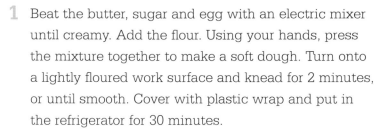

pirate face cookies

MAKES 30

2 cups confectioners' sugar

1 to 2 tablespoons water

2 to 3 drops red food coloring

30 large plain round cookies

4 licorice strips

10 blue jelly beans, cut into thirds

10 red jelly beans, cut into thirds

15 black jelly beans, halved lengthwise

1 Combine the confectioners' sugar and water in a small bowl. Stand the bowl over a saucepan of simmering water and stir until smooth. Remove 1 tablespoon and tint with red food coloring, and set aside. Spread the cookies evenly with the white frosting.

2 Make the pirate faces while the frosting is still wet. Cut the licorice strips into semicircles for the bandanna. Cut the licorice for mustaches and any leftovers can be used for the eye patches. Use the jelly beans for the eye, mouth, and patch. Make the dots on the bandanna, using the red frosting. Store the cookies in the refrigerator until needed.

martian cookies

MAKES 10

1/2 cup unsalted butter, softened

1/2 cup sugar

1 egg

2 cups all-purpose flour

1 cup confectioners' sugar

3 tablespoons hot water

4 drops green food coloring

5 licorice allsorts, thinly sliced

20 jelly beans, halved

5 gummy candies, cut into 4 pieces

1 To make the cookies, beat the butter, sugar, and egg with an electric mixer until creamy. Add the flour.

2 Using your hands, press the mixture together to form a soft dough. Turn onto a lightly floured work surface and knead for 2 minutes, or until smooth. Cover with plastic wrap and refrigerate for 1 hour.

3 Preheat the oven to 350°F. Brush a large baking sheet with melted butter or oil. Roll out the dough between sheets of waxed paper to 1/4 inch thick. Cut into shapes, using gingerbread-people cutters. Put the cookies on the baking sheet and bake for 15 minutes, or until golden. Leave to cool.

4 Sift the confectioners' sugar into a bowl. Add the water and food coloring, and stir well. Dip the front of each cookie into the frosting. While the frosting is still soft, decorate the cookies, as shown, with the candies.

teddy bear cakes

MAKES 12

1 (12-ounce) box butter cake mix

3½ ounces semisweet chocolate chips

1 cup chocolate-hazelnut spread

9 ounces honey-flavored mini teddy cookies

2 tablespoons colored sprinkles

1   Preheat the oven to 350°F. Lightly grease 12 standard muffin cups with oil.

2   Prepare the butter cake mix according to the directions on the box. Fold the chocolate chips into the mixture.

3   Spoon the mixture into the prepared cups. Bake for 15 minutes, or until firm and golden brown. Allow to stand in the muffin pan for 5 minutes. Remove the cakes and cool on a wire rack.

4   Spread each cake with the chocolate-hazelnut spread. Place five teddy cookies around the edge of the cakes. Decorate with colored sprinkles.

chocolate truffles

MAKES 24

1/4 cup unsalted butter

4 tablespoons whipping cream

9 ounces semisweet chocolate, chopped

3 1/2 ounces semisweet, milk or
white chocolate, grated

1   Combine the butter and cream in a small saucepan.
Stir over low heat until the butter has melted. Bring
to a boil and remove from the heat immediately.

2   Place the chocolate in a heatproof bowl and pour in
the hot cream mixture. Cover the bowl for about
1 minute and then stir until the chocolate has melted
and the mixture is smooth. Cool in the refrigerator.

3   Roll heaping teaspoons into balls. Roll the balls in the
grated chocolate. Place the truffles on a foil-lined
baking sheet and refrigerate until completely firm.

cactus juice

SERVES 8

1/2 small cucumber, sliced

4 cups apple juice

1 tablespoon honey

2 cups chilled lemonade

2 cups soda water

1 Place the cucumber in a large bowl with the apple juice and honey. Stir to combine. Cover and refrigerate for at least 1 hour.

2 Pour into eight glasses and add the lemonade and soda water. Top with ice cubes.

foaming craters

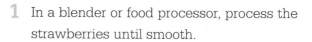

SERVES 8

9 ounces strawberries

8 scoops vanilla ice cream

lemonade, to serve

1 In a blender or food processor, process the strawberries until smooth.

2 Divide puree evenly among eight tall glasses.

3 Place a scoop of vanilla ice cream in each glass and top with lemonade, being careful not to overfill the glass. Serve immediately.

jungle juice

SERVES 8

3 1/2 cups unsweetened pineapple juice

3 cups apple juice

16 ounces canned unsweetened crushed pineapple

3 cups chilled lemonade or ginger ale

candied cherries, to garnish

1 Combine the pineapple juice, apple juice, and crushed pineapple in a large bowl. Stir to combine. Cover and refrigerate for at least 1 hour.

2 Pour into eight glasses and add the lemonade or ginger ale. Garnish with cherries.

fruit punch

SERVES 10

1/2 cup orange juice

15 ounces canned fruit salad

juice of 1 orange

juice of 1 lemon

3 cups chilled lemonade

fresh fruit, such as raspberries, blueberries, apple, orange, cantaloupe, and honeydew melon, to garnish

1 Combine the orange juice, fruit salad, and the fresh orange and lemon juices in a bowl.

2 Stir lightly to combine. Cover and refrigerate for at least 1 hour.

3 Just before serving, add the lemonade. Garnish with fresh fruit.

poison potion

SERVES 1

1 tablespoon lime syrup

1 tablespoon raspberry syrup

lemonade, to serve

1 scoop chocolate ice cream

1 Pour the lime and raspberry syrup into a large glass. Top with the lemonade.

2 Place the chocolate ice cream on top.

3 Allow to stand for 1 minute before serving.

pineapple cream

SERVES 2

16 ounces canned undrained crushed pineapple

1 cup pineapple juice

1 cup coconut milk

pineapple slices, to garnish

1 Combine the crushed pineapple and pineapple juice in a large bowl.

2 Slowly add the coconut milk, whisking continually until well blended.

3 To serve, pour into tall glasses over plenty of ice cubes. Garnish with pineapple slices. Serve immediately.

chocolate-mint dream

MAKES 2

4 scoops chocolate-mint ice cream

1½ cups whole milk

chocolate jimmies, to serve

1 Put 2 scoops of the ice cream and the milk in a blender and blend until smooth.

2 Pour into two tall glasses. Top each glass with a scoop of ice cream and chocolate jimmies. Serve immediately.

piña colada

MAKES 2

1½ cups pineapple juice

1 banana

½ cup canned coconut milk

½ cup ice cubes (optional)

1 Put all the ingredients into a blender and blend until smooth.

2 Pour into two tall glasses to serve.

index

This edition published in 2009 by Andrews McMeel Publishing, LLC. All rights reserved. Printed in China. No part of this book may be used or reproduced in any manner whatsoever without written permission except in the case of reprints in the context of reviews. For information, write Andrews McMeel Publishing, LLC, an Andrews McMeel Universal company, 1130 Walnut Street, Kansas City, Missouri 64106.

First published in 2007 by Murdoch Books Pty Limited Australia
Pier 8/9, 23 Hickson Road, Millers Point NSW 2000

Ready, Steady, Spaghetti copyright © 2007 by Murdoch Books Pty Limited.
09 10 11 12 13 MUB 10 9 8 7 6 5 4 3 2 1

ISBN-13: 978-0-7407-8087-5
ISBN-10: 0-7407-8087-5
Library of Congress Control Number: 2008935052

www.andrewsmcmeel.com

Chief Executive: Juliet Rogers
Publishing Director: Kay Scarlett

Design Manager: Vivien Valk
Design: Alex Frampton
Project Manager: Jane Price
Editor: Gordana Trifunovic
Production: Alexandra Gonzalez
Photographer: Michele Aboud
Stylist: Sarah DeNardi
Food Preparation: Julie Ray and Simon Ruffell

ATTENTION: SCHOOLS AND BUSINESSES

Andrews McMeel books are available at quantity discounts with bulk purchase for educational, business, or sales promotional use. For information, please write to: Special Sales Department, Andrews McMeel Publishing, LLC, 1130 Walnut Street, Kansas City, Missouri 64106.

The publisher and stylist would like to thank Typhoon, Rhubarb, French Bull by Jackie Shapiro, The Source, Villeroy & Boch, Marie Claire Paris plateware, Specklefarm Ribbons, Maxwell & Williams, Design Mode International and Spotlight for lending equipment for use and photography. Thank you to all the models: Felix, Ava, Ruby, Mia, Luca, Elena, Josie, Joe, and Inez.

IMPORTANT: Those who might be at risk from the effects of salmonella poisoning (the elderly, pregnant women, young children, and those suffering from immune deficiency diseases) should consult their doctor with any concerns about eating raw eggs.